SUFFOLK
STRANGE BUT TRUE

SUFFOLK
STRANGE BUT TRUE

ROBERT HALLIDAY

The History Press

This book is dedicated to three Suffolk sisters:
my aunts, Pat Morris and Margaret Stanworth,
and my mother, Joan Halliday

First published 2008
Reprinted 2011, 2012

The History Press Ltd
The Mill, Brimscombe Port
Stroud, Gloucestershire, GL5 2QG
www.thehistorypress.co.uk

British Library Cataloguing in Publication Data.
A catalogue record for this book is available from the British Library.

ISBN 978 0 7509 4704 6

Typesetting and origination by The History Press Ltd.
Printed in Great Britain by Marston Book Services Limited, Didcot.

CONTENTS

INTRODUCTION &
ACKNOWLEDGEMENTS

I have spent much of my life in Suffolk, since moving to Bury St Edmunds in 1966, and have found the history, architecture and countryside a constant source of amazement, as well as inspiration. I hope this book will help develop the understanding of some of the many interesting facets of life in this beautiful county. This book would be much shorter and poorer were it not for many dedicated people in county-wide or local organisations who have worked hard to maintain the places and customs mentioned here.

Many thanks are due to the following: the staff at the Suffolk Record Office who have, as always, proved ever-helpful suppliers of information; Julian Ackland of the Pin Mill Sailing Club for information on the Thames Barge Race and a photograph of the barges in sail; Bob Carr of the Suffolk Archaeological Unit for a photograph of Basil Brown; Mike Chester, keeper of Porcelain at Lowestoft Museum for a photograph of Lowestoft Porcelain and information on the museum and its history and contents; the Kentwell Estate Office for a photograph of Kentwell Hall; Sarah Friswell of St Edmundsbury Cathedral for a photograph of that building; Julia and Stephen Mael for a photograph of and information about the Long Shop Museum at Leiston; Bob Pawsey for a photograph of Gedding Hall and the last herd of Suffolk Dun Poll Cattle; and John Telford-Taylor of Mendlesham for a brilliant photograph of the Boy Bishop. Other people who deserve thanks include Derek Andrews and the Revd Judith Andrews (no relation) of Hollesley for supplying information on beating the bounds at Hollesley; Hannah Deverson of Brandon Town Council for information on the gunflint industry; Jane Haylock for an informative tour of Hadleigh Town Hall; David Johnson, local historian of Acton, for information on that village; Karoline Kennedy, who first showed me the war memorial in St Edmund's Place in Bury St Edmunds; Chris Lamb of Lavenham for insights into that town's history; Dr John Ridgard for many ideas, and for first drawing my attention to Goodwyn Barmby; John Sutton, for information on the royal palaces at Newmarket; Barry Wall for all things Sudbury and Long Melford; Dr Ann Williams, formerly of the North London Polytechnic and tutor for my B.A. degree, for observations on the story of St Edmund and allowing me to publish them.

Insights were provided by members of *Bury Heritage Guides*; Jeremy Hobson; Duncan MacAndrew; Alan Murdie; Peter Northeast; Nigel Russell; Adriana Sascombe-Welles; Andrew Snowdon and Roy Tricker.

1

UNUSUAL LIVES

Redwald

A list of people who shaped Suffolk's character and history might start with Redwald, an Anglo-Saxon king of East Anglia and the first native Suffolk person of whom we have personal knowledge. Rising to prominence in the seventh century from a power base on the south Suffolk seaboard, he became *Bretwalda*, a position awarded to either the senior, most powerful, or most respected Anglo-Saxon king. Archaeology indicates that Ipswich was established at this time, suggesting that he ruled a prosperous and enterprising realm.

Redwald accepted Christianity, but could not reject his queen's ancestral Nordic religion, and installed Christian and pagan altars in a temple at his palace. Edwin, an exiled Northumbrian prince, took refuge at Redwald's court. When King Ethelfrid of Northumbria wanted Redwald to kill Edwin Redwald's wife, he said it was dishonourable to kill a guest: instead, Redwald led an army against Ethelfrid. They met in battle and although Redwald's son, Regnhere, was killed in combat, Redwald was victorious and installed Edwin as king of Northumbria. It is a pity that we do not know more about Redwald's wife: she must have been a forceful and persuasive woman.

In 1938 archaeology gave Redwald a new fame with the excavation of a burial mound at Sutton Hoo. Built over a great ship, it contained royal regalia and gold and silver treasures from all parts of Europe. Many objects displayed Nordic religious symbols, but some included Christian imagery, suggesting devotion to both beliefs. The acid soil had destroyed the body, but it is impossible to conclude that the person buried here was anyone other than Redwald. The discovery revised historical and archaeological opinions of Anglo-Saxon England, previously thought of as a poor, impoverished society; this showed that it was a land of wealth and splendour.

St Edmund

No book on Suffolk would be complete without a mention of St Edmund. In 869, a Viking horde, The Great Army, landed in East Anglia, led by a chieftain called Ivar. The *Anglo-Saxon Chronicle* says it camped at Thetford and defeated and killed Edmund. His armour bearer later described his death to Dunstan, a monk who became Archbishop of Canterbury, who

The martyrdom of St Edmund, as depicted on a medieval misericord (tilt-up seat) in Norton Church.

told it to Abbo of Fleury, a monk who wrote it down. Ivar took Edmund to a location called Haeglisdun (meaning 'holy place') and offered terms: to remain as king under Viking overlordship, sharing his treasury and estates with the Vikings. Edmund said that as a Christian, he could never submit to a pagan. Accordingly, he was tied to a tree, scourged, shot with arrows and beheaded. The death was dated to 20 November, which remains St Edmund's Day. Edmund's followers, seeking his remains, heard calls of 'here, here' and found a wolf guarding his head. To tie a person to a tree, shoot him with arrows and behead him was a way of sacrificing a prisoner to Odin. Norse belief said that Odin visited the world of men disguised as a wolf, so the episode of the wolf might suggest that Odin wished to reject the sacrifice and make amends for Edmund's death. Edmund's refusal to submit in the face of defeat turned him into a hero figure who sacrificed himself for his kingdom. The motif of a king sacrificed on a tree holds great symbolic power, as in the crucifixion of Jesus, Charles II's escape from his enemies by hiding in an oak tree, or the Buddha's enlightenment under the Bo tree testify. Edmund's remains were moved to Bedereceworth, which was renamed Bury St Edmunds (Bury meaning 'burgh' or fortified town, rather than burial place). Haeglisdun was often identified as Hoxne, until Dorothy Whitelock, a leading Anglo-Saxon scholar, argued that the modern version of this name would be Hellesdon. In 1978, Stanley West, the county archaeologist, found a field called Hellesdon at Bradfield St Clare, and suggested that Edmund was martyred there: the location's closeness to Bury makes this hypothesis rather attractive.

Edmund was regarded as England's patron saint until he was replaced by St George. In 2006, the *East Anglian Daily Times* initiated a campaign to reinstate him: a partial victory was gained in April 2007 when Suffolk County Council proclaimed Edmund patron saint of Suffolk.

Suffolk and America

Suffolk people have played an important role in the development of America. These include Thomas Cavendish, the third person to sail around the world, after Ferdinand Magellan and Francis Drake. His family owned Grimston Hall in Trimley, where he was baptised in St Martin's Church. At twenty-five, he captained a ship in Walter Raleigh's expedition to Roanoke in Virginia. Although the fleet was destroyed in a storm, Thomas established a reputation as a naval commander by navigating his ship safely to the Caribbean.

Contemporary engraving of Thomas Cavendish.

In 1586, aged twenty-six, Thomas planned a trip around the world with 123 men in three ships, the *Desire*, the *Hugh Gallant* (built on the Orwell) and the *Content*. Crossing the Atlantic, he navigated the Pacific coast of America, plundering Spanish settlements and capturing several valuable cargo ships, before exploring the Chinese seaboard. Yet, he does not emerge as a wholly romantic figure: he tortured captives and quarrelled with the crew of the *Content* over the division of spoils; they sailed away and were never seen again. Thomas led another voyage in the *Desire*, but this was plagued by disease and bad weather. Arguing with his officers, and only able to control his crew by brutality, his physical and mental condition deteriorated until he died near the equator.

Bartholomew Gosnold belonged to a family who owned land in Otley and Grundisburgh. He married Mary Golding of Bury St Edmunds and their children were christened in St James's Church (now the cathedral). Mary's family had connections with merchants who backed foreign voyages, and in 1602, Bartholomew captained an expedition to North America in the *Concord* with thirty-two men. They explored the Massachusetts coast, naming Cape Cod and finding an island whose beauty so impressed Bartholomew that he named it Martha's Vineyard, possibly after his mother-in-law or his daughter. The voyage set the route for the Pilgrim Fathers and provided William Shakespeare with material for the *Tempest*. In 1607, Bartholomew left his family to command a ship, the *Godspeed*, in the expedition which established Jamestown. He showed some ability as a leader of the new colony (frightening off an Indian raiding party by firing a cannon over their heads), but the colonists suffered from disease and starvation. Bartholomew died after six months, but he had played a key role in creating Jamestown, the first permanent English settlement in America.

John Winthrop, lord of the manor of Groton, was a leading Suffolk puritan. In 1629, he led over 600 people in eleven ships from Ipswich to join the Puritan settlers in New England, the largest single expedition in the New England migration, over a quarter of whom came from Suffolk. Governor of Massachusetts for thirteen years, John Winthrop played an important role in forming the colonial government and setting up Harvard University.

His son, also called John Winthrop, who was born in Groton and educated at Bury St Edmunds Grammar School, was interested in alchemy (which should be seen as an effort to understand what is now called science, rather than a desire to turn base metal to gold). Following his father to New England, he founded New London in Connecticut, which he envisioned as a centre of alchemical research: medical studies took place there. Setting up America's first ironworks, John Winthrop the younger could be regarded as the father of North American science and industry.

John Yonges was the son of Christopher Yonges, vicar of Southwold and Reydon. Also becoming a priest, he emigrated to New England, settling at Salem in Massachusetts. In 1640 he and 138 members of his congregation moved to Yennycock on Long Island, which they renamed Southold, after Southwold; the first permanent English settlement in New York State, where he served as minister for the rest of his life.

Three Suffolk Writers

Robert Bloomfield, 'the Suffolk poet', was born in Honington in 1766. Soon afterwards his father died, but his mother gave him a sound education. At eleven he started work on a farm at Sapiston, but he proved unsuited for heavy labour, and went to London to become a shoemaker. Here he composed *The Farmer's Boy*, based on his memories of rural life. In three

In memory of
Captain Bartholomew Gosnold
explorer and 'prime mover'
behind the first permanent English
settlement in North America at
Jamestown, Virginia,
where he died 22 August 1607
Also of his family
buried in this churchyard:
his wife Mary (d. 1665);
her parents
Robert and Martha Golding
(d. 1611 and 1614);
and his daughter Martha (d. 1598)
hence Martha's Vineyard
1602

A memorial to Bartholomew Gosnold, unveiled on the wall of the ruined charnel house in Bury St Edmunds churchyard on the 400th anniversary of his death and the founding of Jamestown.

years it sold 30,000 copies, the most successful book of English verse then published. Robert described life from the perspective of Giles, a farm boy, who is introduced with the lines:

> T'was thus with Giles, meek, fatherless and poor,
> Labour his portion, but he felt no more . . .
> Strange to the world he wore a bashful look,
> The fields his study, nature was his book.

This must have been a self-portrait, as Robert had lost his father and was physically small, but intellectually active.

Unable to escape contemporary literary conventions, Robert wrote *The Farmer's Boy* with a classically influenced phraseology and metre that can sound stilted and artificial (although showing that he was widely read). Nevertheless, it was the first time that a member of the English rural working class wrote a description of life as experienced by himself and his fellows. Robert's later poems included interesting anecdotes about Suffolk life and folklore, but were progressively less successful. Finding that many people in Suffolk either resented his success or expected money from him, he forsook his native county, spending his last years in Bedfordshire, where he died in reduced circumstances. Yet he left an important legacy: John Clare was inspired to write his highly regarded and influential rural poetry after reading Robert's verses. Robert also made Aeolian harps: one, in Moyse's Hall Museum in Bury St Edmunds, is considered the finest and most important example in existence.

Arthur Young was born in 1741 to a landowning family at Bradfield Combust. Passionately interested in the new developments of the Agricultural and Industrial Revolutions, he conducted innumerable agricultural experiments using old and new methods (one of his books

Contemporary engraving of Robert Bloomfield, 'the Suffolk poet'.

describes over 1,000). For example, he planted crops in different conditions, cultivated fields with different implements and fed his livestock varying diets, keeping meticulous records of the results. He started a journal, *Annals Of Agriculture*, providing practical information on new farming methods, which circulated widely (George III contributed articles on management of the royal estates). When the Board of Agriculture was set up, Arthur was the unanimous choice for its first secretary. Although he went blind in old age, he actively pursued his duties until his death. Arthur Young's writings were the most important single factor in promoting and developing the ideas of the Agricultural Revolution in Britain, for which it is impossible to exaggerate his importance in the history of modern farming.

M.R. James was inspired by his Suffolk heritage to write ghost stories. Montague Rhodes James, or *Monty*, as friends called him, was the son of the rector of Great Livermere. From childhood, he enjoyed visiting historic buildings and studying old books. Going to Cambridge University, intending to become a clergyman, he proved such a brilliant student that he was invited to join the university staff. Writing over 200 studies of medieval art and manuscripts, he became one of the most honoured and respected scholars of his age.

After studying a collection of historic manuscripts in Brent Eleigh Church, Montague wrote a story called *Canon Alberic's Scrapbook*. He read this to some friends at Christmas who were so impressed that he wrote more for subsequent Christmases. *Oh Whistle And I'll Come To You My Lad* described the sinister events that follow the discovery of an object on the golf course at Felixstowe (renamed Burnstow). *The Ash Tree*, recounting the revenge of a woman hanged for witchcraft, was set in a thinly described Livermere. *A Warning To The Curious* described events that follow a man who finds an Anglo-Saxon crown near Seaburgh (really Aldeburgh). At the end of his life he wrote *A Vignette* describing a personal experience at Livermere. Although M.R. James published little more than thirty stories, he drew on an extensive knowledge of folklore and history to avoid obvious horror or evil, but inexorably

Arthur Young's tomb in Bradfield Combust churchyard, designed as a cenotaph to celebrate his services to Britain.

draw the reader into a build-up of uncanny forces. Often best read aloud, they can benefit from repeated reading for greater impact, and have been acclaimed as the best ghost stories in the English language. In 2001, Beryl Dyson, a Livermere resident, published a pamphlet, *A Parish With Ghosts*, describing fourteen supernatural apparitions seen in the village, suggesting that M.R. James grew up in an area where paranormal phenomena are common.

Elizabeth Squirrell, a Suffolk Enigma

The story of Elizabeth Squirrell, 'The Shottisham Angel', who apparently lived for five months without eating or drinking, forms one of the strangest episodes in the history of Victorian Suffolk. The daughter of a Shottisham tradesman and the granddaughter of a Baptist minister, Elizabeth could read by the age of five; at eight she could recite pages of books from memory. When she was twelve she was infected by a spinal disease, after which her appetite disappeared; for a year she only swallowed small doses of milk and sugar. During this time she claimed to have lost the senses of sight and hearing, but to have had visions of angels. A glass tumbler by her bed made ringing noises, which were thought to be angel communications. From May 1852 she stopped eating and drinking altogether, but lost little weight. In August a committee, including doctors and clergymen, examined Elizabeth. Two nurses said they never saw her eat or drink in two days, although she used a parasol to shade herself from the heat. Eight committee members then watched her in pairs. After six days, two of them claimed to find soiling in her bedclothes that suggested food consumption, and to have seen her parents passing her food behind the parasol, whereupon the investigation broke

The denouement of Oh Whistle and I'll Come To You My Lad, *set in a Felixstowe hotel.*

up in confusion. Her case was debated in a public meeting in Ipswich Corn Exchange on 29 September, when several respectable figures affirmed full belief in the genuineness of her case, while sceptics ridiculed what they believed to be their credulity. One committee member, the Revd William Addington Norton, rector of Alderton, published a supportive work about Elizabeth, including poems and prose she had written. Although she used religious imagery that could sound artificial, she showed great powers of expression, especially for a fourteen year old. By the end of 1852, the Squirrell family had attracted such animosity that they left Shottisham. Some people tried to set up a fund to initiate legal action against their detractors, although no case came to court. Elizabeth gradually resumed food consumption; she appears to have married and lived into the twentieth century. Medical science generally agrees that no human could survive for five months without eating or drinking, but some people have lived on minimal or unconventional diets for long periods, and if Elizabeth was pursuing a fraud, she managed to dupe many people for a long time.

George Ellis

There can be no doubt of the duplicity of George Frederick Wilfred Ellis, who fraudulently became rector of Wetheringsett. Born in the Midlands, he became a teacher at a Roman Catholic school. He then approached the bishop of Truro, claiming to be an ordained Roman Catholic priest who wished to join the Church of England. He was given several posts as a curate, ending up at Wetheringsett, where he married the patron of the living's daughter. He soon became rector there, with an annual stipend of £800. George was a popular clergyman for five years, until some people either investigated or developed suspicions about his past. In 1888 he was arrested for conducting a wedding service while not legally authorised to do so. He stood trial in Bury St Edmunds, where it was shown that anybody who had checked his story could easily have found that he had not been ordained as a Roman Catholic priest, or even studied for the priesthood. Never speaking during his trial, he was sentenced to seven years' hard labour. An Act of Parliament had to be passed to legalise the marriages he had performed. After leaving prison, he is believed to have run a boarding house: it would be interesting to know whether the charm and plausibility he must have possessed served him well in this profession.

Goodwyn Barmby

John Goodwyn Barmby is little known, yet he invented an ideology that influenced the lives of everybody on the planet. Born in Yoxford in 1820, he never used his first name. At seventeen, Goodwyn became involved in Owenism, a popular radical doctrine, and Chartism, a movement which championed full adult suffrage. He spoke about these subjects locally and at national rallies, even arguing that women should be allowed to vote. Visiting Paris in 1840, he suggested a new name to describe the revolutionary ideals of the time: *Communism*. The first person to use this word, Goodwyn returned to England to pursue his Communist agenda, advocating a form of democratic communal lifestyle, incorporating a deep reverence for Christianity (he envisioned a national communist Christian church), which he promulgated in poems, pamphlets and journals.

The year 1848 was marked by revolutionary upheavals, most of which collapsed. After this, Goodwyn abandoned communism to become a minister in the Unitarian Church.

In 1879 he retired to Yoxford, where he died two years later, probably never imagining how the expression 'communism' would acquire a wholly new meaning. His Unitarian beliefs precluded a Church of England funeral, and he was buried in Framlingham cemetery. When I asked about his gravestone, the cemetery caretaker had no knowledge of Goodwyn Barmby and had to find the grave from the cemetery register. It seems ironic that while Karl Marx's grave in London's Highgate cemetery is world famous, the grave of the man who invented communism stands unknown in Suffolk.

The little known gravestone in Framlingham cemetery of Goodwyn Barmby, the inventor of the term 'communism'. The inscription reads 'In memory of Goodwyn Barmby preacher and poet and true worker for God and his fellow men died at Yoxford 8th October 1880 aged 60 years.'

Basil Brown

Basil Brown was Suffolk's most important archaeologist. The son of a tenant farmer at Rickinghall, he left school at twelve, but continued to study widely, publishing *Astronomical Atlases, Maps And Charts*, a comprehensive and original study, even though he possessed nothing more elaborate than a 2in telescope. Teaching himself about archaeology, he excavated several sites for Ipswich Museum. This led Edith Pretty to ask him to investigate some mounds near her house at Sutton Hoo. Basil uncovered a ship burial containing grave goods, identified as those of King Redwald. Within a few days a team of experts, the cream of the British archaeological establishment, was convened to take over the excavation. Although Basil was somewhat sidelined, his expertise provided subsequent archaeologists with an excellent base to work from. Excavating into his seventies, Basil encouraged young people to take an interest in archaeology, enlisting their help on his sites; and nobody has been able to fault his excavation techniques at Sutton Hoo or elsewhere; a brilliant achievement for anybody, let alone a self-educated archaeologist.

Basil Brown, Suffolk's greatest archaeologist, who lived at Rickinghall for most of his life.
(By permission of the Suffolk Archaeological Unit)

Suffolk Heroines

Margaret Catchpole has frequently been called the 'Suffolk Heroine'. A servant to John Cobbold, an Ipswich brewer, she saved two of his children from accidents, and his family gave her a basic education. But she stole one of John Cobbold's horses, riding to London in 7½ hours. Apprehended, she was sentenced to death, but the Cobbolds appealed on her behalf, and her punishment was commuted to transportation to Australia. Margaret scaled the walls of Ipswich Gaol with a clothesline, but was reapprehended on the coast, while trying to flee by boat. In Australia, she became an exemplary member of society: a shopkeeper and nurse, writing letters to England which are important historical sources about life in the penal colonies.

John Cobbold's son, Richard, who was only three when Margaret was transported, became rector of Wortham, where he wrote *The History of Margaret Catchpole*, a novelisation of her life, which included a romantic liaison with Will Laud, a sailor turned smuggler, depicting her theft of the horse and prison escape as attempts to elope. Richard described Margaret as bright and attractive, although posters printed after her escape described her as short, pockmarked and capable of disguising herself as a man. Richard also devised a happy ending when she married a Suffolk friend who had emigrated. They raised a family who became sufficiently wealthy to consider buying Kentwell Hall, but decided to stay in Australia. Richard's book, which could be regarded as 'The great Suffolk novel', has frequently been dramatised (most recently by the Eastern Angles Theatre Company) to give Margaret literary immortality.

We have seen how King Redwald's wife influenced Suffolk's history. Other Suffolk women have also made an impression on history. Alice de Bryene was lady of the manor of Acton. Born Alice de Bures in the fourteenth century, she married Sir Guy Bryene, who died eleven

The Cobbold family home on St Margaret's Green in Ipswich, from where Margaret Catchpole stole the horse upon which she rode into literary immortality.

years later, leaving her with two daughters and estates in Acton. We can recreate one year in Alice's life because of the survival of her *Household Book*, her accounts between 1412 and 1413. Recording every expenditure to the nearest halfpenny, for precise itemization, it rather outstrips *Bridget Jones's Diary*, outlining one year's comings and goings and shopping activites in a medieval lady's household. Daily meals and guests are recorded; her cousins Margaret Sampson and Agnes Rokewode were frequent callers, bringing their children. Her half-brother Sir Richard Waldegrave made eleven visits: once he sent his minstrel the day before – was this for a special feast? Every Saturday a merchant arrived with household provisions: the accounts always record an outgoing of a halfpenny on bread for the merchant's horse. We can even see Alice de Bryene, for she was buried in Acton Church under a beautiful memorial brass nearly 5ft long, the first Suffolk woman with whom we can make eye contact.

Alice de Bryene's brass in Acton Church, from a rubbing by the Revd Henry Tyrrell Green of Santon Downham. Notice the lapdog by the hem of her skirt. (By courtesy of Acton P.C.C. and the Suffolk Institute of Archaeology)

Catherine Buck was the daughter of a Bury St Edmunds yarn maker who ran his house as something of a literary salon. Henry Crabb Robinson, the Bury-born journalist, described her as the most eloquent woman he had met, after Madame De Stael, saying that she introduced him to the ideals of the French Revolution. At twenty, Catherine met Thomas Clarkson, the anti-slavery activist, and they married in St Mary's Church in Bury. Moving to the Lake District, she and Thomas became lifelong friends with William and Dorothy Wordsworth and Samuel Taylor Coleridge, helping to develop their literary careers. Sadly, Catherine was struck by ill health, causing her and Thomas to return to Suffolk. They eventually settled at Playford, where Catherine set up a village school and entertained Marie Louise, the exiled queen of Haiti. Catherine and Thomas lived to see the abolition of slavery in the British Empire; at the end of her life, she was visited by Harriet Beecher Stowe, author of the American anti-slavery novel, *Uncle Tom's Cabin*.

Three sisters, Millicent, Agnes and Elizabeth Garrett, members of the Leiston family of industrialists, spent their early lives in Aldeburgh and went on to achieve great things. Millicent was a founder and leader of the campaign for women's suffrage and a pioneer of female education at Cambridge University. Agnes and her cousin, Rhoda Garrett, were the first women to form an interior design company; their ideas were considered as important as those of William Morris. Elizabeth was the first Englishwoman to qualify as a doctor, despite the medical establishment's continual prejudice and opposition. Retiring to Aldeburgh, she became England's first woman mayor.

Evelyn Balfour spent the most productive part of her life in Suffolk. The daughter of the Earl of Balfour, at twenty-one she bought New Bells Farm at Haughley, where she became an anti-tithe activist. Critical of intensive farming methods, she wished to enhance the relationship between food production, soil, living organisms and mankind. This led her to initiate the 'Haughley Experiment', dedicated to organic farming methods (without the use of chemicals). She wrote *The Living Soil*, a vital text on organic subjects and set up the Soil Association, to promote these ideals. Although she left Suffolk in 1970, at the end of her life, a growing appreciation of her ideals led to the award of an OBE. Much of the modern organic movement originated with Evelyn Balfour's work in Suffolk.

2

BY THE ROAD

Monuments

Some structures and objects have been placed beside roads to be seen or used by travellers. Monuments have been erected to recall significant people or events. Rowland Taylor, Hadleigh's first Protestant rector, was burned at the stake at Aldham, a nearby village, during the reign of the Roman Catholic Queen Mary. A stone inscribed: '1555 R TAYLER IN DEFENDING THAT WAS GOOD AT THIS PLAS LEFT HIS BLODE' was covered by a larger obelisk in 1819.

It is often claimed that the Vikings killed St Edmund at Hoxne. St Edmund's Oak was pointed out as the tree on which he was slain (although it had often been observed that it did not appear to be sufficiently old for this honour). When it fell in 1848, a stone cross was erected on the site; this was destroyed by lightning and replaced by a granite cross. It has recently been suggested that the bishops of Norwich, who were lords of the manor of Hoxne, promoted the St Edmund connection to steal some of Bury Abbey's glory. Hoxne residents object to this, and take pride in and care of sites traditionally associated with Edmund. There is a story that Edmund hid from the Vikings under the Goldbrook Bridge, when a wedding party spotted him and betrayed him. Since then, it has been unlucky to cross the bridge on the way to a wedding, and people attending weddings in the church try to avoid it. The nearby village hall sports plaques showing Edmund's martyrdom, and is topped by his statue.

Every town and village in Suffolk contains a war memorial to the dead of two world wars; these poignant structures can often recall fading memories of the sacrifice of many young men. One of the tallest (possibly *the* tallest) in the country is a 127ft-high Corinthian column between Elveden and Mildenhall. Commissioned by Edward Cecil Guinness, Earl of Iveagh of Elveden Hall, and designed by Clyde Young, it was erected in 1921. At the meeting point of Elveden, Eriswell and Icklingham, three plaques on the pedestal list forty-seven dead from these villages, each standing within the relevant parish. Its remote situation makes it particularly dramatic, although the effect is now slightly spoilt by the proliferation of motor cars running past along the A11.

The county's smallest war memorial is a wooden tabernacle on a wall in St Edmund's Place in Bury St Edmunds. It was put up by the residents of neighbouring homes in honour of ten men from the street who served in the First World War. The houses where they lived have been pulled down, but the memorial is not wholly forgotten, as British Legion poppies can always be seen on it.

Rowland Taylor's memorial on Aldham Common near Hadleigh.

Elveden War Memorial, England's tallest war memorial, in memory of the dead from the parishes of Elveden, Eriswell and Icklingham.

Suffolk's smallest war memorial, honouring the men from St Edmund's Place in Bury St Edmunds who served their country during the First World War.

The author standing beside the 'tithe war' memorial at Elmsett, placed opposite the parish church to embarrass the ecclesiastical authorities.

Between 1931 and 1934, Suffolk was the setting for many actions in the 'tithe war', a conflict which disrupted local life, even if it did not cause any fatalities. Payment of tithes to the Church continued as a rent charge on some English farms. When the Depression made payment difficult, farmers organised to resist. Sidney Westren, an Elmsett farmer, refused to pay, and his property was distrained. He thwarted several attempted seizures: for example local farmers came and disrupted efforts by contractors to remove his cornstacks. When bailiffs finally raided Sidney Westren's farmhouse, he caused Elmsett Church permanent embarrassment by erecting an 8ft-high concrete memorial opposite the churchyard gate inscribed:

TO COMMEMMORATE [sic] THE TITHE SEIZURE AT ELMSETT HALL OF FURNITURE INCLUDING BABY'S BED AND BLANKETS HERD OF DAIRY COWS EIGHT CORN AND SEED STACKS – VALUED AT £1200 – FOR TITHE VALUED AT £385.

Over 140 cattle and pigs were distrained to pay for tithe at Hall Farm at Wortham, owned by Rowley Rash and his wife, Doreen (better known by her maiden name, Doreen Wallace, under which she wrote many novels set in Suffolk). The Rashes and their workers barricaded Hall Farm, digging trenches around it and blocking paths with tree trunks and agricultural machinery. Forty of Oswald Mosley's British Union of Fascists (or Blackshirts) camped at Hall Farm, hoping to gain rural support by assisting tithe resistance, but they were escorted away by 100 policemen. Hall Farm was eventually raided by forty operatives, accompanied by eighty police officers. In a planned operation, the barricades were scaled or broken, and the animals were loaded into boxes before being removed, but the seizure attracted over 1,000 spectators, including journalists and newsreel cameramen, bringing extensive publicity to the anti-tithe movement. Rowley and Doreen erected a memorial on a side-road, ½ mile west of Wortham parish church, inscribed:

THE TITHE WAR 134 PIGS AND 15 CATTLE (VALUE £702) SEIZED FOR TITHE FEB 22 1934

Continued agitation led to the tithe's replacement with a land tax, to be gradually phased out, but inflation so reduced it that most payments ceased in the 1960s.

Roadside Graves

Certain suicides were buried at crossroads at parish boundaries; the practice was only abolished in England in 1823. This may have derived from a belief that the suicide's ghost would be unable to find its way back to its home. 'The Boy's Grave', which resembles a well-kept grave, lies at a crossroad on the edge of Moulton, on the road from Newmarket to Kentford. My grandmother, Margaret Halliday (née Starling) who was born nearby in Ashley (Cambridgeshire) in 1878, and lived to be ninety-six, spoke of a shepherd boy who thought he had lost a sheep. Afraid of being blamed for its theft, and either hanged or transported to Australia, he hanged himself. When the sheep were counted, none were missing – he had miscounted. He was buried at the crossroad; since then, gypsies have cared for the grave in secret. A recent story says that a local squire hired a gypsy boy as a shepherd. The local house-dwelling population resented this; they stole a sheep and let the gypsies take the blame. The squire drove the gypsies away and the boy hanged himself in shame. However, the story is at variance with gypsy life: gypsies are excellent horsemen, but they do not keep sheep. Since

The Boy's Grave on the road between Newmarket and Kentford.

I first saw the grave in about 1960 it has always been covered with flowers, although non-gypsies have often admitted to tending it.

Dobbs's Grave gives its name to Dobbs Lane at Kesgrave. Mr Dobbs (his first name has long been forgotten) is said to have hanged himself and been buried here. At an uncertain date some men drinking at the Bell Inn (still standing in Kesgrave) wondered if there was a burial there. Taking some spades and shovels to open the grave, they found a skeleton. One of the party took a tooth, which he kept on his watch chain. A Dobbs family appears in Kesgrave parish registers during the eighteenth century, and the grave appears on the 1805 Ordnance Survey Map of the area, when a footpath crossing Dobbs Lane formed a crossroad. Early in the twentieth century, a concrete headstone and footstone were placed over the grave, and it was recently enclosed with metal railings.

Thomas Mills's tombhouse, a small rectangular building, stands in Station Road in Framlingham. Thomas Mills left money to build an almshouse in Framlingham, and asked to be buried in the grounds; possibly, as a Baptist, he did not desire burial in the graveyard of the parish church. He left his fortune and business interests to the care of his servant, James Mayhew, who was also buried there.

Market Crosses, Lockups, Stocks and Whipping Posts

Market crosses were focal points of trading communities. In 1501, William Jacob, a clothier, left money to build the impressive stone cross in Lavenham Market Place, asking that it be modelled on that at Cambridge. Mildenhall was granted the right to hold a weekly market and an annual fair in 1412, so it seems plausible that the market cross there, an open hexagonal structure, was built to celebrate the rise in the town's fortunes.

Debenham village green was once a market-place and is surrounded by impressive buildings showing that it was once an important trading centre. A two-storey market cross with an open ground floor was built at the north end of the market. In 1668, Sir Robert Hitcham founded a boys' school at Debenham; this was accommodated in the upper storey. The ground floor had been enclosed by the nineteenth century and the building now houses a commercial art gallery and an architect's office.

Dobbs's Grave in Dobb's Lane, Kesgrave.

Thomas Mills's tombhouse in Station Road, Framlingham.

Mildenhall market cross.

  Penal structures often stood near a market cross or a church, perhaps symbolising the power of Church or State to regulate trade or uphold the law. Miscreants might be punished by the humiliation of public display in the stocks. In Suffolk, these consisted of an upper and lower beam with six leg holes, held together with a hinge and padlock at opposite ends. People could be manacled and flogged on whipping posts, which had wrist irons attached. A fine example of stocks with a central whipping post stand outside the churchyard gate at Ufford. At Redlingfield, stocks stood on the village green, but since they were showing signs of decay, they were moved to the porch of the parish church. It could be argued that removing them from their original location detracts from their historic value, but it may be necessary to ensure their preservation. At Saxtead, the county's finest surviving stocks and whipping post stand in the church porch. They display the inscription, 'Fear God and honour the king' (presumably to remind you of the punishment awaiting you if you did not!). There is another set of stocks in the church porch of South Elmham St Margaret Church. At Thorpe Morieux, a whipping post on a small triangular green near the parish church was adapted as a signpost, and now supports the village sign. James Maggs's *Southwold Diary* suggests that the town stocks there were last used in 1850, when somebody spent six hours in them for being drunk and disorderly. The stocks and whipping post which stand on Bartholemew Green outside Southwold churchyard wall were made in 1984, copying photographs of the lost originals. Stocks by Pakefield Chruch were long thought to be lost, but were re-discovered in a barn in 2010 and replaced by the churchyard gate.

Left: *Debenham market cross.*

Below: *The stocks and whipping post at Ufford.*

Lockups were prisons for the temporary imprisonment of minor felons, such as drunkards or vagrants, until they sobered up or could be removed or taken to court. Boxford village lockup is a twin-chambered white brick building. It was later used to house the village fire engine and is now a bus shelter. Woolpit's lockup stood in the village's central market-place, but the parish council had it moved to Green Road. Perhaps it was thought too unattractive for the centre of the village, but too historically important to be demolished. Lockups in Sproughton and Bramford stand between houses in the High Street; the one at Sproughton is now disused, but the Bramford lockup has become a storeroom and emergency exit for

The lockup at Sproughton.

the village's British Legion. The village lockup at Stoke-by-Nayland, a rectangular, red-brick building with a pyramid roof, stands in the north-west corner of the churchyard.

Bungay was devastated by a fire in 1688; as rebuilding began a new Butter Cross was built, from which agricultural produce could be sold. Until the Victorian era, this incorporated a lockup with a small dungeon underneath, 6ft high and wide. The stocks once stood nearby: these have long since vanished, but there are wrist irons on one of the southern pillars, which must have been used as a whipping post.

The market at Walton had vanished by the eighteenth century. A small, hexagonal market cross opposite the church was converted into a lockup in 1795, at a cost of £46 3s 3d. Sold in 1851, it ended up in the grounds of the Chiswick Polish Company in London. In 1957 the vicar of Walton had it returned and rebuilt beside the churchyard, to become Suffolk's most historic bus shelter. The churchwardens' accounts record that a whipping post and stocks were made in 1747 and 1795 for 15s 9d and £1 6s 5½d. They originally stood beside the cross, but have now been moved to the Felixstowe Museum at Landguard Fort.

The Butter Cross at Bungay.

*The Cage (formerly
the market cross) by the
churchyard at Walton.*

Water Supplies

Public water supplies have often stood by the road to provide sustenance for travellers.
A red-brick Elizabethan conduit on Long Melford Green was funded by Sir William Cordell,
the first post-Reformation owner of Melford Hall. Water was piped from a spring to supply
this and the Hall. The doorway is permanently locked, although there is now little inside.
A conduit near the church was abandoned, as it was thought that burials in the churchyard
contaminated the water. A smaller, octagonal Elizabethan conduit house at Rushbrooke was
built by the Jermyn family, owners of the sadly lost Rushbrooke Hall.

    The Borough Well, in Borough Well Lane at Bungay, stands under a Tudor brick arch.
Traditionally called the Roman Well, a pump was installed in the seventeenth century. It
remained the town's principal water supply until the nineteenth century. When the Bungay
Society restored it, Roman potsherds were found in the bore.

    There was a spring on the parish boundary of Henham and Blythburgh, north of the
Blythburgh-Halesworth Road (once known as 'Springhole' or 'Spring Lane'). At the start of
the Victorian era, Charlotte Rous, Countess of Stradbroke, who lived at Henham Hall, had a
stone canopy erected over it, with stone benches inside. Cups were once chained to the walls

The conduit at Rushbrooke.

for people to drink from. It came to be known as 'The Lady's Well', and it was the subject of a poem by Agnes Strickland, the Southwold poetess and author. (Legends stating that it was a sacred spring, associated with the saintly King Anna of East Anglia, supposedly buried at Blythburgh, are probably only of recent origin.)

There is an impressive early Victorian town pump, topped by a gas lamp, near the Market Cross in Mildenhall. Town pumps in Saxmundham Market Place and on Aldeburgh Town Steps were made by Garretts of Leiston in 1838 and 1840. The pump in Southwold Market Place was provided by the Mayor, J.E. Grubbe, in 1873. Made in the Child family's foundry in nearby Child's Passage, it is a rather jolly affair, with a spout in the form of a dolphin, and herrings decorating the top. The pump in Halesworth market place, with an attractive stone column, was built for Queen Victoria's Golden Jubilee, over the town well, which had occupied this site from the sixteenth century. In the past year, to revive village traditions, a new public village pump has been placed on the village green at Great Livermere.

The pump at Southwold,
taken when a jazz band
was playing in the market.

Animal Drinking Fountains

From the Victorian age, public-spirited people had roadside drinking troughs made for the benefit of animals, especially horses; the survivals are often used to grow flowers. A stone horse trough by the railings of St Peter's Church in Sudbury bears an inscription saying it was given by Alice Mary Brown. It has achieved literary immortality through Dodie Smith's children's novel *101 Dalmatians* (adapted as a well-known film by the Walt Disney studios). Pongo and Missis, the parent Dalmatians, are travelling to Hell Hall in a remote part of Suffolk, to rescue their puppies from the villainess, Cruella De Vil. Arriving in Sudbury, they stop to drink here as the clocks strike midnight.

OUIDA MEMORIAL, BURY S? EDMUNDS.

The Ouida Memorial in
Bury St Edmunds.

Marie Malcolm, a Scottish noblewoman, altruistically paid 100 guineas for a marble horse trough in Haverhill. Made by E.M. Green, a local craftsman, it was unveiled on Haverhill's central Cangle Junction in 1900. Circular, supported on pillars, with upper and lower bowls for horses and dogs, and a mug chained to it for people, it was known as 'The Fountain'. Removed during a road-widening scheme, it ended up in Wood Green Animal Sanctuary at Godmanchester. Haverhill Town Council and the Local History Group bought it back and reinstalled it in Queen Street.

The Ouida Memorial stands at the junction of Horringer Road and Vinery Road in Bury St Edmunds. Ouida was the pen-name of Marie Louise Ramé. Born in Bury, she fantasised that her ancestors were exotic continental adventurers. Leaving the town at eighteen, never to return, she wrote elaborate romantic novels, which were best-sellers in their time. She was a great animal lover and some of her books speak out against animal cruelty; one of her better novels was the historical romance, *A Dog of Flanders*. Ouida spent her last years in Italy, reduced to penury by her extravagance, starving herself to feed her dogs. She stated that she had no wish to be remembered in Bury, as she identified with her French ancestors rather than her mundane Suffolk birthplace; yet on her death in 1908, the *Daily Mirror* organised a fund-raising campaign to erect this memorial which was designed by Ernest Gillick and

The Daniel Cooper Memorial (also known as 'the birdcage') at Newmarket.

constructed by Hanchett's, a Bury firm of stonemasons. An inscription says: 'Here may God's creatures whom she loved assuage her tender soul as they drink'. Unfortunately, the memorial now stands somewhat neglected and forlorn and rather hidden from view.

Daniel Cooper, a member of an eminent Australian family, joined the Newmarket horse-racing fraternity (his horse, Flair, won the thousand guineas). After his death in 1909 his widow, Harriet, acquired land at the west end of Newmarket High Street on which she erected a Portland stone memorial. Adorned with racing insignia, it was intended to be a horse's drinking fountain. Twenty-three feet high, it was called 'the birdcage', from which the nearby street is called Birdcage Walk.

Marker Stones

Prominent or large stones may be ascribed significance, as the continuing fascination of such monuments at Stonehenge or Avebury shows. Large rocks do not naturally occur in Suffolk, so stones of unusual size can seem particularly impressive. A limestone boulder, 4ft wide and 3ft high, stands on Hartest village green. One tradition says that it was pulled from the neighbouring parish of Somerton by forty horses (Suffolk Punches?) in 1713, to celebrate the end of the War of the Spanish Succession, although it is possible that its discovery then was co-incidental. Village children used to see how many could stand on it at once, but it could never fit more that twenty, unless one strong lad twisted the rules by supporting another boy on his shoulders. A smaller boulder stands across the road marking the entrance to Place Farm.

The Gipping Stone, a glacial erratic in Bramford, gives its name to Gippingstone Lane. Other glacial erratics have been built into the church, in the lower stages of the tower and the south wall of the chancel, while two smaller stones lie in the churchyard, north-east of the chancel.

A glacial erratic 2ft high stands beside the Plumber's Arms pub on the Bury-Haverhill road, which crosses the parish boundary between Denston and Wickhambrook. Nothing is known about its history; it may have marked the parish boundary.

Some stones are ascribed religious connections. Various stories claim that the 'Preaching Stone' in Old Market Street at Mendlesham was used as a platform by monks or friars, and even John Wesley. Father Philip Gray says prayers there during revived festivals in January and May. Other stones are (quite erroneously) associated with human sacrifice, such as that on Stonecross Green at Whepstead, which has been called 'The Baal Stone', although it was the base of a medieval cross. Horace Barker's *West Suffolk Illustrated* (1907) says a stone on Rush Green at Harleston was believed to mark the spot where Protestant martyrs were burned during Mary Tudor's reign (although there is no evidence that this took place). The Druid's Stone, in front of St Mary's Church in Bungay, is over 2ft high. Its name reflects a belief that it holds pre-Christian significance. There is a tradition that if one runs around it twelve times, the Devil appears. This may be a joke, as when I tried to do this I became so dizzy that I lost count of my circuits.

A stone cross base in Risbygate Street in Bury St Edmunds, in front of the West Suffolk College, marked the boundary of the Liberty of St Edmund. There is a hollow in the top. Legend says that during a plague in Bury, this was filled with vinegar which people dipped

The limestone boulder on Hartest village green.

The Gipping Stone at Bramford.

their coins in to stop the plague spreading – a primitive form of disinfectant. (The College Theatre is named 'The Vinegar Bowl Theatre' after this.) Had vinegar been placed in the hollow, it would soon have been diluted by rain and precipitation or dried up by the sun. Perhaps the tale represents belief in the curative power of the cross.

The Witches' Stones, in Belle Vue Park, at Lowestoft, a cairn of rough stones cemented together, has been capped by an anchor. They may be the base of a Tudor warning beacon, where fires, visible at sea, were lit in times of emergency. In 1662, Amy Denny and Rose Cullendar, two Lowestoft women, were hanged for bewitching the children of Samuel Pacy, a local tradesman. There is a story that Amy Denny sat on the stones shouting abuse at passers-by, although this is not mentioned in contemporary accounts of her activities.

Stone Farm, on the Bury Road at Stanningfield, is named after some unusually large boulders by the farm entrance. (Coincidentally, Stanningfield means 'stony field'.) Some large boulders on Hunts Green in Donkey Lane in Lawshall appear to have only been placed there recently, showing a continued interest in such unusual objects.

The Blaxhall Stone, at Stone Farm in Blaxhall, is 5ft across and 2ft high. Tradition holds that the farm foreman dropped it here when it was only the size of two fists, and since then it has grown to its present size. It is probably a glacial erratic, but its appearance in this part of Suffolk would have seemed so unusual that this story may have been devised to explain its presence here. On the other hand, people might like to measure it when they visit Blaxhall to see if it does grow!

3

SEASONAL CUSTOMS

Seasonal customs, marking special days or times of year, can enliven the passage of time and provide continuity to the rhythm of life. While some have faded away as society has changed, others have developed a new vitality.

Carlow's Charity, Woodbridge

In 1738 George Carlow bequeathed his property in Woodbridge for charitable purposes. He asked to be buried in his garden and for bread to be distributed from his grave on the anniversary of his death (3 February). Although the garden is private property and wholly inaccessible to the public, until at least the 1960s, the rector of Woodbridge distributed loaves from Carlow's Grave every year on 3 February, with teachers taking local schoolchildren to receive them. The custom has now passed out of use, but there are hopes that it might be revived.

Valentine's Day

In nineteenth-century Suffolk, children went to local houses on Valentine's Day to sing for pennies and treats. The popular song took the form:

> Good morrow Valentine,
> Curl your hair as I do mine,
> Two in front and two behind
> And so good morrow Valentine.

The practice declined at the end of the century. In 1901, the *East Anglian Miscellany* said it ceased at Thwaite two years previously. When Horace Barker's *West Suffolk Illustrated* described the custom at Fornham St Martin in 1907, it was regarded as unusual. Nicholas Everitt continued the tradition at Broad House at Oulton some years after that. In 1940 the *Bury Free Press* described how 108 local children and London evacuees sang *Good Morrow Valentine* at Barton Mere (a house between Great Barton and Pakenham) for Brigadier Moray Quayle-Jones, who gave each child three pence and a bun; he said that 150 years previously they each had a penny (and some beer)! The custom ended after the Brigadier's death in

January 1946. When visiting Barton Mere at a Red Cross Garden Open Day in 1999, I met some elderly people from Pakenham who remembered singing there. The custom continues at Somerleyton, as Penny and Bun Day: on the schoolday nearest 14 February, children from the village primary school still sing and present cards at Somerleyton Hall, receiving fifty pence and an iced bun each.

Good Friday Skipping

In several places in England it was customary for adults to go skipping with ropes on public open spaces on Good Friday. Such places included Hardwick Heath near Bury St Edmunds. An article in the *Bury Free Press* of 10 April 1970 says that men turned the ropes while the women jumped. The Rootsweb website (http://www.archiver.rootsweb.com) contains the recollections of Robert (Bob) Palmer, born in Bury in 1905, posted by his daughter-in-law, Christine Palmer. Bob recalled that there would be 'dozens of people there all skipping all afternoon'. Peggy Bridges, a friend of mine, informs me that her grandparents moved to Bury in 1919, after which her father, John Bridges, then aged five (later the schoolmaster at Shimpling), went to Hardwick Heath for the skipping, but the practice ceased in the 1920s.

The Race of the Bogmen

While repairing the roof at Boyton Hall Farmhouse at Great Finborough in 1975, farmer Trevor Waspe found an agricultural workers' contract dated 1897, updated annually until 1915. Trevor discovered that in 1897 Joseph John Hatton, the farmer at the time, hired a team of villagers to plough the farm. On receiving the traditional advance payment, they went to the pub, got drunk and started a brawl. In anger, Joseph sacked them. Word got around that a new team was wanted, and on Easter Monday, some men from Haughley arrived at Boyton Hall asking for work. By then, Joseph's anger had relented and he had re-engaged the Finborough team. Somebody suggested that the contract be thrown into the air, and the teams race with it to the Chestnut Horse Pub, the contract being awarded to whichever side carried it through the pub door first. Teams from Great Finborough and Haughley repeated the race every Easter Monday, regarding it as an enjoyable start to the agricultural year, but it was forgotten with the First World War.

Trevor Waspe revived the race in 1976 between two teams of six men from Great Finborough and Haughley, and this has continued every Easter Monday since. Boyton Hall Farm stands on a hill, so spectators can watch progress across the fields. Now run purely for entertainment, the race is organised in a great spirit of fun, with regular free-for-alls as participants try to gain hold of the contract, and a fearsome tussle outside the Chestnut Horse. The day includes an egg-throwing contest and egg and spoon races in Church Road.

Long Melford Fair

In 1235, Henry III granted the Abbot of Bury the right to hold a fair at Long Melford for three days from Trinity Sunday. Moved to Whitsun in 1330, this still takes place on the green. Until the early twentieth century, it was known for the sale of horses, and was popular among gypsies who camped nearby when the fair was in progress; however, it is now a funfair.

The Race of The Bogmen at Great Finborough, 2007.

Beating the Bounds at Hollesley

The tradition of 'beating the bounds' of the parish was revived at Hollesley in 1966 as a protest against encroaching development. When there was a scheme to build over part of the former common, the villagers beat the bounds to show its extent. They were helped by small earth mounds known locally as *dills* that had been created to mark the boundary. Beating the bounds now takes place every second year (on years ending with an even number) on Rogation Sunday (the fifth Sunday after Easter) when villagers take shovels to rebuild the mounds. The vicar sets them off with a prayer. Children are 'bounced' on the mounds so they will remember their location. Hollesley parish boundary runs through the US airbase at Sutton. Once there was a standoff when perimeter guards had not received advance notice of the event and confronted the villagers with loaded guns. Luckily, senior officers on the base knew about the tradition, and once it was realised they were not Soviet spies, the procession continued.

The Jankyn Smyth Memorial Service

The Jankyn Smyth memorial service, held in St Mary's Church in Bury St Edmunds since 1481, is the longest continually held endowed religious service in the world. Jankyn (a diminutive of John) Smyth was the alderman of Bury six times between 1423 and 1463, and established almshouses which are still in operation. One of the abbey's most resented privileges was a tax known as the Abbot's Cope, which the town had to pay when a new abbot was appointed. Jankyn set up an endowment to pay this, relieving the townspeople of the burden.

Jankyn Smyth's will asked that a requiem mass be said for his soul in St Mary's Church on the anniversary of his death, to be attended by town officials and residents of his almshouses, who would be regaled with 'cakes and ale' afterwards. Jankyn Smyth's benevolence turned him into a local hero, and the service continued as a Protestant ceremony after the Reformation. It is now held on the Thursday nearest 28 June (the date of his death). Residents of Jankyn Smyth's almshouses and members of St Edmundsbury Borough Council attend, before retiring to the Guildhall for refreshments.

The Pin Mill Barge Race

A Thames sailing barge race is held at Pin Mill every summer. Pin Mill, a very attractive riverside hamlet at Chelmondiston, on the south bank of the Orwell, is a venue for boating enthusiasts and maintains a thriving sailing club.

Thames sailing barges were the last sailing vessels to operate commercially in Britain: a few carried cargoes between Norfolk and Kent until the 1940s. Barge owners held an annual race on the Thames. This last took place in 1962, and there were fears that a nautical tradition would end when some enthusiasts suggested that a barge race should be held at Pin Mill. This proved so popular among spectators and participants that it has continued every year, on a Saturday in late June or early July. (The precise time and date varies each year, as the race has to coincide with a high tide, but times can be obtained from Pin Mill Sailing Club.)

Thames barges at the annual Pin Mill Barge Race. (Julian Ackland of Pin Mill Sailing Club)

Minden Day

During the Seven Years War, on 1 August 1759, the British and French armies met at Minden. The Suffolk Regiment (then known as 'The Twelfth Foot') and five other infantry regiments repelled three French cavalry charges and a line of French infantry. Roses were growing on the battlefield, and the soldiers picked these to wear on their headgear. The Suffolk Regiment, which now forms the first battalion of the Royal Anglian Regiment, parades at Gibraltar Barracks in Bury St Edmunds, the former regimental headquarters on 1 August, while the Regiment's Old Comrade's Association holds its reunion and parade on the Sunday nearest to that date. On both occasions participants wear a yellow and a red rose in honour of the Battle of Minden.

The Polstead Gospel Oak Service

Polstead's Gospel Oak stood in the grounds of Polstead Hall, clearly visible from the churchyard. At the start of the twentieth century, it was 36ft in circumference. Tradition maintained that monks preached there before the church was built; it has been claimed that these included St Cedd (although this would have made it over 1,300 years old). The Revd Francis John Eld, rector of Polstead, held an open-air service beside it on 3 August 1902, and this has become an annual event. Sadly, the Gospel Oak collapsed in November 1953, but a sapling, which had sown naturally, continues as the venue for the service, which takes place on the first Sunday in August.

The British Open Crabbing Championship

The British Crabbing Association has organised a crab fishing contest at Walberswick every year since 1981. Open to all for a £1 entry fee, contestants fish for the heaviest crab with a weighted line, using their choice of bait. Suitable fishing tackle can be bought on the day for a small charge. (Nets and hooks are forbidden, and crabs are caught and kept alive, so contestants must bring or buy buckets to keep them in.) Maroons are fired at ninety-minute intervals to signal the start and finish of the contest.

The 2007 contest attracted over 700 entrants. Oscar Kane from Kent, aged eight, caught a 5¾ ounce crab for the first prize of a gold medal, a silver salver and £50. Silver and bronze medals, with £30 and £15 for 4¾ ounce and 3¾ ounce crabs, went to Isabella Brinton and George Ellis, aged three and fourteen. (The record, set in the first contest, was for a 7¼ ounce crab.) Every participant receives a pot of Shippam's crab paste. All money raised goes to local charities, and the crabs are returned live to the sea at the end of the contest. The contest is held on a Sunday in August. The precise date and time, which varies to coincide with a high tide, can be obtained from the British Crabbing Association or the Southwold Tourist Information Centre.

Boxing Day Hunting

The hunting of small birds and animals on Boxing Day is a custom whose passing will probably not be regretted. John Brand's *Popular Antiquities* (1813), a pioneering study of British folklore, mentions 'a credible person born and brought up in a village near Bury St Edmunds' who said that local youths hunted squirrels and owls at Christmas. Robert Forby's *Vocabulary of East Anglia* (1830) and John Gage's *History Of Thingoe Hundred* (1838) (the area west of Bury St Edmunds) said that hunting squirrels at Christmas with sticks and stones continued at that date, but suggested that it was declining in popularity.

Variants of the 'Cutty Wren' custom took place on Boxing Day in Suffolk. Suffolk writer Alan Jobson's *An Hour Glass On The Run* (1959) included the reminiscences of his grandfather, Mr Barham, a farmer at Middleton, whose earliest memory was the winter of 1814. Mr Barham recalled how village youths killed a wren. They fastened this to a bunch of holly and ivy on a broomstick and knocked on the doors of village houses, asking for pennies or treats, with the song:

> The wren, the wren the king of all birds,
> Saint Stephen's Day was caught in the furze;
> Although he is little, his family is great –
> I pray you good landlady, give us a treat!

As St Stephen was the first Christian martyr, his festival is held on 26 December. It is unlikely that many village boys knew this, suggesting that the rhyme could date from the Middle Ages. Claude Ticehurst's *History of the Birds of Suffolk* (1932) said the custom continued into living memory at Harleston, where it was called 'stag hunting' and the bird was called a 'stag'.

In 1994, the Old Glory Molly Dancers, a folk dance group, formed at Rumburgh. In collaboration with Suffolk folklorist Pete Jennings, they revived the Cutty Wren tradition at Middleton. Before readers get too alarmed, it should be emphasised that they never even contemplated killing a wren, but decided to use a carved wooden bird instead. (When I spoke to members of Old Glory about the practice, they wondered if wrens, which are small and elusive, were often killed, or if boys simply caged them for the day, or just pretended to have killed them.) At about 9 in the evening, the Old Glory Molly Dancers arrive in procession at Middleton, led by a drummer beating a single beat, while a man in agricultural labourers' clothes sweeps the way for a Lord (in top hat and tails) and Lady (a man rather unconvincingly dressed in a green gown), followed by the Wren Bearer, carrying a wooden wren on a pole garlanded with holly and ivy. They perform at the Bell public house, while a 'box man' asks for contributions with the rhyme:

> I have this little box under my arm
> Tuppence or threepence should do you no harm
> So its up with the kettle and down with the pan,
> Pray give us a penny to bury the wren.

Revival of Customs at Mendlesham

Father Philip Gray, the vicar of Mendlesham, has revived medieval festivals to signify the Christian year. In January he holds a 'Plough Sunday' service which includes Morris dancing. In May (the month of Mary) he crowns one of the village girls as the May Queen (representing the Virgin Mary, whose statue in the church is also crowned), and holds a service that includes garland dances. At Halloween he blesses pumpkins and witches' hats and brooms to show the power of God over evil. As part of the Christmas celebrations, he has revived the Boy Bishop

The Boy Bishop at Mendlesham in 2005.
(John Telford-Taylor)

ceremony, a medieval ceremony in which a boy is initiated with a scaled-down replica of a bishop's costume, to preside over a service, accompanied by a chaplain, who is also selected from the village boys. When I spoke to Father Philip about this he said, 'I think faith should be great fun', arguing that the angel announcing Christ's nativity said, 'I bring you tidings of great joy'.

Southwold Seasonal Customs

Henry VII granted Southwold a charter in 1489, which included the right to hold a three-day fair from Trinity Sunday. After proclaiming the fair in 1922, the mayor, Alderman A.J. Critten, took the first ride on the roundabouts. Since then, the mayor, councillors and town clerk have taken the first ride on the fairground amusements. Organising the fair became increasingly difficult, as the date of Trinity Sunday varies every year, and in 1997, the town authorities decided to hold it from the last Thursday in May to the following Sunday. Since it no longer coincided with Trinity Sunday, it was renamed 'Charter Fair'.

Above: *Southwold's Charter Fair, 2007.*

Right: *A demonstration of an umbrella that recycles water at the 2007 Southwold Flying Egg Festival.*

Alternative umbrellas at the 2007 Southwold Flying Egg Festival.

Southwold's spectacular medieval parish church is dedicated to St Edmund. In 1908, the vicar started the tradition of giving local schoolchildren buns on St Edmund's Day (20 November), which came to be known as 'Sticky Bun Day'. This ceased, but was revived in 1989, as part of the celebrations marking 500th anniversary of the town's charter. The mayor and town councillors give local schoolchildren a bun each, after which they attend a short service in the church. One of the ceremony's more admirable aspects is to make the children feel that they play a role in Southwold's historical continuity.

Southwold's most recent, and most amazing custom is the Flying Egg Competition. By its own definition, 'our challenge is to find exciting and bizarre alternatives to mundane practical objects that no one ever really notices' and 'to explore the link between imagination and functionality and promote the use of recycled materials'. In 2001, local author Linda Sonntag thought of holding a contest to devise a more attractive and ecologically friendly alternative to her rotary clothesline; however, she cannot recall any particular reason for choosing the name 'flying egg'. Working examples had to be made and displayed in Southwold High Street. The maker of the entry judged the best, a retracting clothesline in a black panther's head, received a £1,000 prize. Since then, there have been contests to make an alternative bird table, weather-vane, deckchair and clock. The winning entry is now partly chosen by spectator vote, and there are prizes for the best young contestants. The 2007 contest for an alternative umbrella attracted seventy entries, several made by schools and youth organisations. Some examples incorporated devices for recycling water, while there was a jungle umbrella, and an umbrella on which watercress could be grown. Halesworth artist Rachel Roft won first prize for an origami umbrella showing a child protected from a bomb blast. Let's hope that the fantastic Flying Egg competition continues for many years to come.

4

ARCHITECTURAL CURIOSITIES

Despite the continuing efforts of some local authorities and planners to render Suffolk indistinguishable from any other part of the world (as the monstrous new Cattle Market complex in Bury St Edmunds shows), the county still possesses a wide and varied architectural heritage, and many organisations are working to conserve and maintain this, with great success.

West Stow Anglo-Saxon Village

An important architectural experiment is being carried out at West Stow Country Park. After archaeologists uncovered an Anglo-Saxon settlement, buildings of timber, thatch, wattle and daub were built over the excavated post holes and foundation trenches to make practical recreations of Anglo-Saxon houses to study the domestic conditions they provided. This is the first time that Anglo-Saxon buildings have been constructed over archaeologically established foundations, and the experiment is providing archaeologists and historians with a wealth of inspiration.

Moyse's Hall

Moyse's Hall in Bury St Edmunds, built in the twelfth century, is the county's oldest house. Its vaulted undercroft is the only domestic structure in England containing both circular Romanesque (or Norman) arches and pointed Gothic arches. There is a long-standing tradition that Moyse's Hall was originally a Jews' house: certainly, there was a Jewish community in Bury during the twelfth century, and since Jews were often financiers and money-lenders, they built stone houses to safeguard their wealth. When the Borough Council planned to turn it into a fire station, Hermann Gollancz, a rabbi, complained that a relic of medieval Jewry should be treated thus. William Spanton, a local artist and photographer, initiated a preservation campaign which mobilised local public opinion to make Moyse's Hall the local museum in 1899. Strangely, there are now plans to move large sections of the Borough Museum's collection from Moyse's Hall to West Stow, a move which takes museum re-organisation too far. While West Stow forms a brilliant recreation of an Anglo-Saxon village, let us hope it can be realised that certain buildings are just right for displaying certain collections.

Reconstructed Anglo-Saxon houses at West Stow. Members of Stowacynn, the village's Anglo-Saxon re-enactment group, stand in front of The Hall to the left. The Living House can be seen to the right.

The Gothic undercroft at Moyse's Hall.

The ruins of the new abbey church at Leiston, showing the twelfth-century crossing arches.

RUINS OF THE HERMIT'S CHAPEL, LEISTON.

The ruins of the old abbey at Leiston, later converted into a hermitage.

Leiston Abbey

Leiston Abbey was founded in 1183, but the site became waterlogged and prone to flooding, causing the monks to move to a new monastery further inland in 1365. Yet the ruins of the new abbey church incorporate twelfth-century columns and arches: were they reused from the first abbey, or did the monks adapt an existing church? After the Dissolution, a farmhouse was built in the ruins which the Pro Corda Trust now runs as a school for outstanding young musicians: Leiston Abbey thus continues to be a centre for study and inspiration. Some fragments of the first abbey survive near the Minsmere Nature Reserve: John Green, the penultimate abbot, retired here to become a hermit. During the Second World War a pillbox was built inside the ruin. Standing within view of Sizewell Nuclear Power Station, the juxtaposition of the spiritual forces of the Middle Ages and the technological forces of the twentieth century make an uneasy couple.

Clare Priory

Gilbert de Clare founded Britain's first community of Austin Friars at Clare in 1249. Friars lived under monastic vows, but went into the community to preach to and work; the Austin Friars followed rules formulated by St Augustine of Hippo. Gilbert de Clare married Edward I's daughter, Joan of Acre; she was buried in the friary church, as was Lionel, Duke of Clarence, a son of Edward III. After the Dissolution, the priory became a house. In 1953 the owner, Lady Mary Barker, gave it to the Austin Friars – the first medieval monastery in Britain to return to the religious order it was built for. The priory church is in ruins; a large opening near the site of the altar is thought to have been Joan of Acre's monument. Both Leiston Abbey and Clare Priory can be visited all year round, however visitors should respect the privacy of residents' houses.

The west front of Clare Priory.

The Abbey Gate at Bury St Edmunds.

Butley Priory Gatehouse.

The Friary Gatehouse at Sudbury.

Monastery Gatehouses

It is remarkable that after a monastery has fallen into ruin, the gatehouse is often preserved. At Bury St Edmunds, the gatehouses are by far the best preserved buildings from the abbey. The elaborately decorated twelfth-century Norman tower which stood before the abbey church was kept as the bell tower of St James's Church (now the cathedral). The main abbey gate originally aligned with Abbeygate Street (or Cook's Row as it was called until 1792). The townspeople came to resent the abbey's power, and in 1327, they sacked and ransacked it, destroying the gatehouse. As part of their punishment the townspeople had to pay for a replacement. Battering rams, heavy stones and burning tar barrels could have been run down Cook's Row against the gate; to prevent a reoccurrence, the new gate was sited further south, and fortified with battlements, arrow slits and a portcullis.

The largest surviving fragment of Butley Priory is the spectacular fourteenth-century gatehouse. Built with stone from the Yonne Valley in France, a panel over the entrance displays thirty-five coats of arms of families associated with the priory – an impressive statement of authority and influence – placed clearly at the monastery entrance.

There was a small priory at Letheringham. Parts of the church survived as a parish church; the gatehouse, a small fifteenth-century building with a single room above, also survives, although it is now in a derelict condition.

The timber-framed gatehouse of the Dominican Friary in Friars Street in Sudbury became a house after the Dissolution. A stone house to the west, which was once a pub called the Star and Ship or the Hole in the Wall (as there were no windows on the street side), was probably the friary guesthouse to accommodate visitors and passing travellers.

Wolsey's Gate in College Street in Ipswich is the only survival of a spectacular establishment. Thomas Wolsey, the son of an Ipswich merchant, became Archbishop of York

Wolsey's Gate in College Street, Ipswich.

and Henry VIII's chief minister. Pope Leo X made him a cardinal and he twice attempted to be elected Pope. Thomas established the Cardinal's College of St Mary in Ipswich as his memorial in his home town, a school educating boys of promise. Wolsey closed ten monasteries in Suffolk, Norfolk and Essex to endow it, the priory of St Peter and St Paul in Ipswich being used as a temporary premises until appropriately magnificent new buildings could be completed. The nearby chancel of St Peter's Church was removed in preparation for its reconstruction as a magnificent new school chapel. But Wolsey fell foul of Henry VIII because of his inability to secure the king a divorce; his death soon after probably saved him from execution. Henry closed the school, its property was confiscated and buildings demolished (leaving St Peter's in a sad, truncated condition). Only one small side gateway was left. The merits of speculating about history's 'what-ifs' are rather doubtful, but had Thomas Wolsey's plans been realized, Cardinal's College could have become England's largest, most magnificent and most important school, rivalling (or even eclipsing) Eton and Harrow, transforming Ipswich with a magnificent architectural complex and bringing it great fame and prestige.

Gatehouses can be symbolic buildings, advertising the owner's power and authority, and defining spheres of influence. It is interesting to note that when the townsfolk of Bury wished to overthrow the abbey, they destroyed the gatehouse, while the monks reasserted their authority by rebuilding it on a grander scale. Yet after the eventual overthrow of all Suffolk monasteries, several gatehouses were preserved. Could the retention of the Norman tower as the bellower of St James's Church represent the continuity of Christian worship? Did the post-Dissolution owners of monastic property (even unconsciously) wish to show themselves as the inheritor or supplanter of the monastic authority and tradition?

Hadleigh Town Hall.

Hadleigh Churchyard

Hadleigh was a centre of the medieval wool-cloth industry. Its church stands in a large churchyard, bordered by the fifteenth-century Market Hall and the Deanery Tower – a grouping which has been described as Suffolk's cathedral close! The ground floor of the timber-framed Market Hall contained shops; the upper stories were a Town Hall. A southern guildhall wing was added for Hadleigh's five guilds (religious, social and commercial societies); this became a workhouse after the Reformation. The Guildhall roof does not quite align with the walls; it may have been reused from the previous parish church at Hadleigh. Still forming local government offices, this complex demonstrates the wealth that the wool-cloth trade brought the region.

The Deanery Tower or Gatehouse at Hadleigh.

Kentwell Hall. The earlier mansion is just visible to the left. (By permission of the Estate Office)

The rector of Hadleigh received the highest stipend of any Suffolk clergyman. One rector, William Pykenham, who was also Archdeacon of Suffolk and a prominent lawyer, planned to build a residence on similar lines to Oxburgh Hall in Norfolk. Only the gatehouse was completed by his death. It became part of the rectory, and in 1833 the rector, Hugh James Rose, presided over a conference there where a group of churchmen devised plans to issue a series of *Tracts For The Times*, spearheading the Tractarian movement, which reintroduced medieval and Roman Catholic-inspired ritual, practice and architecture into the Church of England, revolutionising Victorian Christianity.

Kentwell and Melford Hall

Long Melford contains two spectacular mansions: Kentwell Hall and Melford Hall. Both were believed to be mid-Tudor, but have now been shown to be even older. Kentwell Hall, a moated mansion, was built for the Clopton family, landowners and wool-cloth entrepreneurs, in the 1430s. Two generations later, in the last quarter of the century, John Clopton had a new hall wing built against this, running east-west; in the mid-sixteenth century the new hall was enlarged with east and west wings, and then being topped with a Long Gallery (since turned into bedrooms). Remarkably, the west wing of the original house survives, standing by the moat, one of the best preserved domestic buildings of this period in England. Since 1971 Patrick Phillips has been renovating Kentwell Hall, organising elaborate historical re-enactments every year. Details of events and admmissions can be obtained from Kentwell Hall.

Melford Hall was a grange of the abbots of Bury. John Reeve, the last abbot, who came from Long Melford, had it rebuilt, perhaps to advertise his wealth and status in his home

Melford Hall.

community. Six towers decorating the building rise from rectangular bases to octagonal turrets. The south front, facing the village, with raised wings and a central 'gatehouse', resembles the main frontage of Thomas Wolsey's mansion at Hampton Court; perhaps the design was an example of contemporary Suffolk clergy 'keeping up with the Joneses'. After the Dissolution, William Cordell, a lawyer, acquired the Hall; he moved the main entrance from the south (facing the Green) to the north (away from the village): adapting it as his house by adding a new entrance. Melford Hall is now opened to the public by the National Trust.

The Ancient House

The Ancient House in Ipswich originated as a fourteenth-century shop and house. After being extended to the south and south-west, George Copping, an Elizabethan merchant, added a west wing, incorporating a Long Gallery. His will specified that nothing should be removed from the house, which may have led to the preservation of three large wall hangings of the labours of Hercules, recently found behind panelling. The Sparrowe family had the spectacular north wing facing the Buttermarket built in 1668, displaying the finest pargetting (ornamental plasterwork) in the country. Scenes show the continents, the giant Atlas supporting the world; the elements of water, earth and air; and St George despatching the dragon in a rustic seventeenth-century setting. The Sparrowes lived here until Victorian times, when it became a printers and bookshop. It is now a shop selling household products; part of its attraction may be that it has been a working commercial premises throughout its history.

The Ancient House at Ipswich.

Detail of pargetting on the Ancient House.

*The Palace House
at Newmarket.*

Newmarket Palace House

James I had a residence built in Newmarket High Street to stay in when enjoying local sporting events, but this cannot have been of a very high standard, as it collapsed after three years. A more substantial Prince's Lodgings replaced it; Charles I last stayed there under house arrest at the end of the Civil War. Parts of the Prince's lodge may remain in the former Palace Yard west of Kingston Passage. On returning to England, Charles II had a new palace built further to the east, around an irregular courtyard. Tradition holds that Nell Gwynn's House in Palace Street is so named as Nell Gwynn accompanied Charles II to Newmarket and stayed there so that they could meet without upsetting court protocol. William IV and Queen Victoria had little interest in horse-racing; the palace was neglected or dismantled, leaving only a pavilion from the south-west corner, which includes a bedroom used by William III. It is now a Tourist Information Centre; during renovation a sash window was found, with counter-balanced wooden frames and original glass – the earliest known example in the world.

Ickworth House. While the east wing (left) was used by the Hervey family for domestic accomodation, the rotunda (centre) contained the state apartments, while the west wing (right) was a hollow shell. Note the lack of chimneys on the west wing.

Ickworth

The Hervey family of Ickworth became Earls of Bristol in 1714. Ickworth House, one of England's largest, most eccentric and unconventional houses, was the brainchild of Frederick Hervey, the 'Earl Bishop'. A younger son of the family, Frederick entered the Church for want of a better career, and was only appointed Bishop of Derry in Ireland through family influence. Paradoxically, he was an exemplary bishop for several years, but he eventually lost interest in Ireland and began touring Italy, where he built up a colossal art collection, before becoming fourth Earl of Bristol after the death of two elder brothers (the first person in England since William the Conqueror's half-brother, Odo, to be a bishop and an earl). In 1795, Frederick envisioned a new mansion at Ickworth, comprising a central rotunda, where the Herveys could live, with two long wings to house his art collection. Mario Asprucci, an Italian architect, designed it, and Francis Sandys, an English architect, modified it for the English climate. But when Napoleon invaded Italy, Frederick's art collection was confiscated. After this, Frederick rather aimlessly toured the Continent (never returning to England). After Frederick's death, his son, Frederick William (who was created Marquess of Bristol) had the building completed. The central rotunda is 105ft high, and the entire house is 600ft long. Frederick's plans were too expensive to complete, and much of the west wing was a hollow shell, only built for symmetry, until its recent conversion into a visitor centre. Ickworth House is now opened to the public by the National Trust.

Bridges

The twelfth-century Abbot's Bridge at Bury St Edmunds was built against the abbey's precinct wall in Eastgate Street, allowing the monks to cross the River Lark without leaving the abbey precinct. External buttresses are perforated by doorways that supported a plank

The so-called 'Packhorse Bridge' at Moulton.

bridge, allowing other people to cross the river without entering the abbey precinct – a design unique in Britain.

At Moulton, two medieval bridges cross the River Kennett, which bisects the village green. The larger, a prominent structure with four arches, has traditionally been called the Packhorse Bridge, although it is wide enough to accommodate a standard medieval cart. A smaller, single-arch footbridge stands to the south. Moulton was granted the right to hold a market in 1298, so these may have been prestige projects, celebrating the village's importance.

Helmingham Hall is unique in Suffolk in being hemmed in by a moat, and only accessible by drawbridges, which have traditionally been raised every night since 1510.

An iron bridge crosses a canalised stream in the park surrounding Culford Hall (now a public school). This was the residence of the Cornwallis family. Recent research suggests that the architect and engineer Samuel Wyatt, who had already worked on Culford Hall, designed the bridge for the Second Marquis Cornwallis in 1803, making it one of the world's oldest iron bridges.

A bridge crossing the Waveney at Homersfield was the first concrete bridge to be built in Britain. Constructed in 1869 for the Adair family of Flixton Hall, its survival is somewhat fortuitous, since it was built as a private venture, and stood at the meeting point of seven local authorities' jurisdictions, so that, as road traffic increased in the twentieth century, it was unclear who was responsible for maintaining or replacing it, and it therefore remained unaltered until its importance was recognised. A new bridge was then built alongside it, and it was restored and converted into a footbridge, after which representatives of the seven local authorities simultaneously cut ribbons to reopen it.

The Orwell Bridge, carrying the A14 from Ipswich to Felixstowe, opened in 1982. Standing 1,400yds long and 78ft wide, it was styled to blend in with the landscape, in a design approved by the Royal Fine Art Commission. Its centre span is 200yds long; at the time of construction the longest piece of pre-stressed concrete in the world.

The bridge at Culford Park, one of the oldest iron bridges in the world.

Theatres

The Rifle Hall in Halesworth was built as a theatre in 1792. After a local clergyman described it as the 'resort of the most worthless characters in existence', Halesworth was rocked by a year-long debate on the vices and virtues of the theatre. It became the headquarters of the local battalion of the Volunteer Rifle Corps (hence its name), and local military organisations continued to use it, building a new façade. It later became a public hall, and theatrical productions are occasionally held there. (A maltings in Halesworth has since been adapted as The Cut Arts Centre, which stages theatrical productions and live entertainment.)

A garrison was stationed at Woodbridge during the Napoleonic Wars. The demand for entertainment led to a theatre being built in 1814, at a cost of £2,000. Giving its name to Theatre Street, within fifty years it had become a school. It is now a furniture store. (Woodbridge has since acquired the excellent modern Seckford Theatre, although it seems sad that this early theatre should not be appreciated.)

The Theatre Royal in Bury St Edmunds is England's only functioning Regency Theatre. It was designed in 1819 by William Wilkins, an architect and a member of a family of East Anglian theatrical impresarios (who later designed the National Gallery in London). He had it built over a slope in the ground, which helped the seats to rise as they receded from the stage. In 1892, it staged the first ever performance of the farce *Charley's Aunt*. Closing in 1925, it became a barrel store for the Greene King Brewery. Eventually, a group of enthusiasts initiated a restoration scheme, and it re-opened under the National Trust's care in 1965. It was restored to something approaching its original Regency appearance, which involved some conjecture, as there were no illustrations to work from. The roof was painted with a diorama of the sky, a gesture to the open-air theatres of classical Greece. It has recently undergone a lengthy restoration to improve its facilities and further restore its Regency character.

Bungay's Fisher Theatre was built for an eponymous family of East Anglian theatrical impresarios. Opening in 1828 as the New Theatre, it only operated for twenty years before being converted into a Corn Exchange. It later became a cinema, a laundry and a government surplus store, before some Bungay residents bought it and initiated a restoration project, after which it reopened as a theatre in 2006.

The Bury Theatre Royal has come to be regarded as one of the finest theatres of any small town in England, putting on a genuinely rewarding and varied programme at a modest cost. In a short time, the Fisher Theatre has also more than proved its worth. Suffolk can be proud of its theatrical tradition, which is as good as any area of England. Since 1982 a brilliant Ipswich-based touring company, the Eastern Angles, have carried provincial theatre to a new level, producing musical dramas about such subjects as the Lowestoft fishing industry, the Sutton Hoo excavations, and the Tithe War, doing much to reveal the region's dramatic potential.

Ixworth Council Houses

Four semi-detached cottages in Stow Road at Ixworth have often been identified as Britain's oldest council houses. Three years after the 1890 Housing of the Working Classes Act empowered local authorities to build houses, Thingoe Rural District Council replaced some unhygienic, badly built houses with new buildings with ¼-acre gardens, an important episode in the history of public housing.

Thorpeness

Thorpeness was the brainchild of Stuart Ogilvie. Inheriting land on the Suffolk coast in 1908, Ogilvie had the idea of turning Thorpe Haven, or Thorpe, a fishing hamlet, into a holiday

The 'House in the Clouds' and the windmill at Thorpeness.

Fantasy buildings at Thorpeness.

village in a 'merrie England' Tudor style. After sketching an outline plan, he enlisted the architects Forbes Glennie and William Gilmour Wilson to realise his design. Every building was constructed to a strikingly different design, although their timber-framed frontages were purely façades over concrete substructures. Local fishermen dug out an existing lake to create 'The Meare', a boating lake (never more than 3ft deep). J.M. Barrie had recently published *Peter Pan*, and several islands recreated such settings as Wendy's House, the Pirate's Cove or the Crocodile's Lair. When a water supply was laid on a large water tower was disguised to look like a very tall house (being called 'The House in the Clouds'), the water being pumped by a windmill which was moved from Aldringham. Thorpeness remained the Ogilvie family's property until quite recently, leading to its preservation as an idyllic garden village, one of England's most surprising and rewarding architectural fantasies.

5

CASTLES AND FORTIFICATIONS

Suffolk is a coastal county, so there has always been a need to defend its shoreline, while military and political developments have led to the construction of castles and military strongpoints across the region. It is not well known that there was a castle at Ipswich. The least documented Norman castle in any English county town, King Stephen besieged and took it in 1153, but even its location is uncertain. Other castles have left impressive remains, as at Clare, where the extensive earthworks of the De Clare family's castle can be seen. The Malet family built a castle at Eye. The last remnants fell out of use in the seventeenth century, but the mound or motte still dominates the town, and the town's main streets follow the outline of the bailey. A royal castle at Haughley was destroyed in a rebellion against Henry II in 1173 and never rebuilt, but the motte survives (although on private land). There was a castle on a natural ridge at Lidgate. The parish church was built within its defences and one can admire the earthworks and some small rubble remains from the churchyard. Castle earthworks at Denham (near Barrow in West Suffolk) have recently been opened as a public amenity with display boards. Other castles and military buildings still stand in various states of preservation.

Burgh Castle

Burgh Castle represents the east, south and north perimeter walls of a Roman shore fort, between 640 and 300ft long. Built at the end of the estuary of the Yare and Waveney (much broader in Roman times), encroachment by the Waveney has since caused the west wall to collapse. It has often been identified with Garionnum, a fort that accommodated a 500-strong cavalry force. The Venerable Bede wrote that St Fursey, a seventh-century Irish monk, established a monastery in East Anglia at a former Roman camp called Cnobheresburg. This has often been identified as Burgh Castle. The Normans later constructed an earth motte in the south-west corner. A Victorian landowner had this levelled, and would probably have demolished the walls to extend his farmland, when another landowner, Sir John Bolieau, bought them to ensure their preservation.

Between 1958 and 1961, areas inside the walls were excavated, when many finds (and by inference the fort itself) were dated to the mid-fourth century AD. An Anglo-Saxon cemetery containing 163 burials lay beside the south wall, but nothing was found to conclusively prove

Burgh Castle.

or disprove monastic activity. (The excavators optimistically identified some circular trenches as monastic cells, but these were in reality only soil marks.) A scarcity of medieval material (and lack of medieval documentation about the site) suggested that the Norman castle was soon abandoned.

It was once believed that Roman shore forts were built for defence against Anglo-Saxon invaders. Recent research suggests that fourth-century Britain enjoyed economic revival, while the Anglo-Saxons only arrived in small groups as colonists, and it is now argued that Burgh Castle could have been a trading and administrative centre.

Bungay Castle

Bungay and Framlingham castles, built in the eleventh centuries, were the principal strongholds of the Bigod family. From 1135, Hugh Bigod exploited Stephen and Matilda's rivalry for the crown to increase his power and become Earl of Norfolk. He reached an accommodation with the next king, Henry II, and rebuilt Bungay Castle after 1163, but joined Henry's opponents in a concerted attack on royal power in 1173. With the Earl of Leicester, he mounted an unsuccessful siege of Dunwich and took Haughley Castle, but the Earl of Leicester's army was obliterated in battle at Fornham St Genevieve, near Bury St Edmunds. Hugh did occupy Norwich, but when Henry entered Suffolk with the royal army, Hugh found himself isolated in Bungay. At Syleham, he submitted and surrendered his castles. Royal engineers were demolishing Bungay Castle when Hugh redeemed it for 1,000 marks (£666 1s 8d). Three years later, Hugh, then aged eighty, died on his way to a crusade. Roger Bigod, the fifth Earl of Norfolk, re-fortified Bungay in 1294, but his death brought the family line to an end. Within a century the castle was described as 'old and ruinous'. Nevertheless, it was so strongly built that when an eighteenth-century contractor called Mickleborough tried to level the ruins, his workmen broke all their tools on it. Elizabeth Bonhote, a local woman, had a house built between the gate towers where she wrote a Gothic romance called *Bungay Castle*.

A central motte can be entered by a gatehouse flanked by round towers, probably built for Roger Bigod. The base of Hugh's keep possesses the thickest walls of any British castle keep, between 18 and 23ft wide. There was a large forebuilding on the north, whose lower level may have been a prison. The keeps of Scarborough Castle in Yorkshire and Bungay contain spiral staircases within a side wall (unlike every other rectangular keep, where this is in a corner), while Bungay's keep is faced with a sandstone found near Scarborough. Clearly the builders of these castles cooperated. In 1933 the ruins were excavated to provide work for local unemployed. In the forebuilding they found an alcove containing a latrine pit (and a wooden toilet seat) but the pit was so deep that they could not reach the bottom. They also found a tunnel cutting through the keep's foundations. Henry II's engineers must have planned to demolish the keep by undermining it before Hugh paid to regain it.

Bungay Castle Trust open the ruins to the public and maintain a visitor centre.

Orford Castle

Orford Castle is Suffolk's most architecturally innovative medieval fortification. The Pipe Rolls, royal audit accounts, show that it was built between 1165 and 1170 at a cost of £1,235 11s 3d, making it the first castle in England whose building history and budget are precisely known. The keep used a new polygonal plan, with three towers extending from the sides. This occupied less space than a rectangular keep, but was stronger and easier to defend, as defenders could fire arrows and missiles over a wider range, and the walls lacked blind corners, could deflect missiles and were harder to undermine. The interior contains three

Some remains of the keep at Bungay Castle can be seen between the gatehouse towers.

Orford Castle.

central circular chambers: an entrance hall, a lower basement (with a well) and a larger upper room. At the time, the legends of King Arthur and his Knights of the Round Table were becoming popular. Could these circular rooms have been an attempt to emulate Arthurian romance?

It is often asserted that Henry built Orford Castle to curb Hugh Bigod, but it seems unlikely that Henry would have permitted Hugh to rebuild Bungay Castle at the same time. Work on both castles began shortly after Henry started his bitter quarrel with Thomas Becket, his

Archbishop of Canterbury and former friend. Becket had excommunicated Bigod, so Bigod and Henry probably saw the archbishop as a common enemy and may have built new castles in case Becket's supporters tried to invade England. In the rebellion of 1173 Orford Castle was garrisoned by twenty knights, although it is unclear if it saw any military action. Yet, despite the importance Henry attached to this castle, he never visited it.

Orford Castle passed into private ownership from the fourteenth century. The keep became an empty shell, but was preserved as a navigation mark and military signal station. Later owners restored it as an eccentric seaside cottage. In the Second World War it served as a military lookout, and a concrete radar platform was placed on the roof, which has been kept to demonstrate its modern military history.

Framlingham Castle

Richard I ('the Lionheart') returned Framlingham Castle to Hugh Bigod's son, Roger, the second Earl of Norfolk, who had it rebuilt as a walled enclosure with thirteen towers, possibly intended to be as much a residence as a fortress. An extensive network of lakes surround the castle. While these could have helped protect the castle and been used as fishponds, it is hard to imagine that they cannot also have been created to beautify the surroundings – an early attempt at landscape architecture, perhaps inspired by the new Arthurian romances.

In the fifteenth century, Framlingham passed to the Howard family, who became Dukes of Norfolk. When the Howards fell foul of Tudor court intrigue, Henry VIII took Framlingham for his son, Edward VI, who held his first court here before presenting it to his sister, Mary. After Edward's death in 1553, several Protestant nobles, led by the Duke of Northumberland, tried to sideline the Roman Catholic Mary from the throne by installing Lady Jane Grey

Framlingham Castle.

Mettingham Castle.

in her place. Mary fled to Framlingham, where she proclaimed herself Queen. The people of Suffolk saw her as the rightful sovereign and flocked to join her. Within a few days, 20,000 of her supporters were camped before the castle; suddenly England's future focused on Framlingham. The Duke of Northumberland marched against Mary, but he could only assemble a much smaller and less committed force. On reaching Bury St Edmunds, he found his position had so weakened that he withdrew, allowing Mary to ascend the throne. Mary returned Framlingham to the Howards, but they came to see it as old fashioned, and sold it in 1635, to become a municipal centre, housing the local workhouse, courtroom and fire station, before falling into decay.

Orford and Framlingham Castles are now maintained by English Heritage, who open them to the public. Both castles incorporate local history museums.

Mettingham and Wingfield

By the fourteenth century, castles were becoming increasingly expensive to build and maintain, but some aristocrats built castle-like houses to symbolise their wealth and prestige. From 1343, John de Norwich, a successful soldier in Edward III's Scottish and French wars, enlarged his family home at Mettingham into a castle by extending around two courtyards. It is uncertain if it would have made a particularly successful military strongpoint (for strategic purposes, it might have made more sense to build it nearer the River Waveney). During the Peasant's Revolt, the local population ransacked it (although it was probably unoccupied at the time). After Mettingham Castle passed to a cousin of the Norwich family who was a nun, it was turned into a religious community. Following Henry VIII's Dissolution, it declined into a farmyard, and adjoining land is still used for agriculture.

Wingfield Castle.

Wingfield Castle was built from 1382 for Michael De La Pole, first Earl of Suffolk and Lord Chancellor to Richard II. The son of a merchant who made a fortune bankrolling Edward III's military campaigns, Michael built Wingfield Castle to display his new-found status. He did not enjoy this for long, as he was blamed for unpopular governmental policies and forced into exile in 1387. The De La Poles married into the Plantagenet royal family, as a result of which they were effectively purged by Henry VIII as potential rivals for the throne. Much of the castle was then dismantled. But in the 1940s it was restored as a residence, and it is now one of the few English castles that is also an Englishman's home.

Mettingham and Wingfield Castles are private property, but their exteriors can be seen from the road.

Landguard Fort

Landguard Fort, built to guard the Orwell estuary, is an unexpected feature of the modern port and holiday resort of Felixstowe. First built in 1626 as a square building with angle bastions, within twenty years there were complaints that it was falling down and the garrison's pay was seven years in arrears. Perhaps it was just as well that it saw no action during the Civil War.

The fort was restored in 1663, which may have been fortunate, for the Anglo-Dutch War started soon afterwards. On 2 July 1667, a Dutch fleet sailed near to the Orwell estuary. Although sandbars prevented the warships from coming too close to the shore, about 2,000 soldiers and marines landed in rowboats on the beach to the north of the fort and attempted to scale the walls with ladders. The garrison, led by Captain Nathaniel Darrell, maintained a rigorous

The sea-facing front of Landguard Fort, Felixstowe.

defence, while two English ships, the *Truelove* and the *Lennox* came and fired at the Dutch. After two unsuccessful assaults over one hour, the Dutch withdrew. The train bands (a local defence force), who had anticipated Dutch raids, mobilised at Walton and marched to Landguard Fort. The Dutch meanwhile had returned to their rowboats, but the tide had gone out, leaving them stranded on the shore. There was a stalemate until after midnight, when the rising tide allowed the Dutch to return to their ships. The garrison at Landguard Fort suffered one fatality and four wounded, including Nathaniel Darrell, who was shot in the shoulder. Although some accounts claimed several hundred Dutch casualties, they probably lost no more than twenty men and perhaps two or three times as many wounded. But both countries were tired of the war and peace was concluded soon afterwards. While small invasion forces landed on the Irish, Scottish and Welsh coasts during the eighteenth century, the Dutch attack on Landguard Fort marked the last occasion that a hostile, foreign army landed on the coast of England.

Ten years later, Landguard Fort was said to be 'in the most miserable condition of any fort in Europe'. In 1717 it was replaced by a new fort slightly to the east, which was rebuilt in 1744, and again after 1871. Colonel George Tomline, the landowner who developed Felixstowe as a port and holiday resort, thought this infringed his rights. As lord of the manor, he claimed an archaic privilege to levy tolls on building materials carried across the foreshore, which he increased from sixpence (2½d) to 2s 6d (12½ pence) a ton. When the War Office refused to pay, he cut off the fort's water supply. The government invoked the Defence Act to purchase the foreshore; Colonel Tomline demanded £40,000 but received rather less than £2,000. The fort was garrisoned throughout the First and Second World Wars, and then monitored Soviet activity until the last troops left in 1957. After a period of deterioration, restoration work was undertaken by English Heritage and a dedicated team of volunteers, who now open it to the public. There is also a local history museum in the adjoining Ravelin Block.

The entrance to Landguard Fort, Felixstowe.

The interior of Languard Fort.

The Southwold Guns

Six cannons face the sea at Gun Hill at Southwold. There is some mystery over their origin: local tradition holds that they were presented by the Duke of Cumberland on his return from fighting 'Bonny Prince Charley' in 1745. Yet the Duke is never known to have come near Southwold, and since the cannons are Elizabethan culverins, they may have been installed here much earlier. Southwold was presented with some artillery pieces for defence in 1569, although these were frequently neglected. After the Spanish Armada, there were further plans to fortify Southwold, although only a small battery was actually built. In 1626, Dunkirkers (pirates from Dunkirk, a port under nominal Spanish control) captured a ship off Southwold and bombarded the town. The townspeople asked the government for more protection, and some cannons were supplied two years later. It seems plausible that the guns are part of either the Elizabethan or Stuart defences. By the eighteenth century they were of limited effectiveness. During the French Revolutionary Wars, defence volunteers complained that they were inoperable. Yet the townsfolk regarded them as private property and refused to remove them during the decommissioning of coastal defences after the Battle of Waterloo. When George IV sailed along the Suffolk coast, he was annoyed that they were fired in his honour, but the townsfolk said they could fire their own guns whenever they wanted. They were fired again when Queen Victoria sailed past, but a salute to celebrate the birth of the Prince of Wales (later Edward VII) tragically caused an explosion which killed the soldier who was operating it. This impressed itself on local folklore, leading to a belief that the guns are haunted by a headless soldier, and they have never been fired since.

German destroyers shelled Southwold in 1917, claiming the guns made it a legitimate military target (luckily no injuries resulted). To prevent a reoccurrence, the guns were removed and replaced by up-to-date (but concealed) artillery. Similar precautions were taken during the Second World War, since when they have stood on the cliff top.

The Southwold Guns.

Martello Towers

In 1793, defenders of a tower on Cape Mortella in Corsica held off the British Navy and inflicted an eye wound on Horatio Nelson. In an amazing example of military improvisation, the British military authorities thought similar towers would make excellent coastal defences and planned to build them in Britain, although construction only began after Nelson's victory at Trafalgar ended any realistic possibility of a Napoleonic invasion. The first towers were built along the South Coast and building on the East Coast followed; 108 had been built by 1808, of which eighteen were in Suffolk – two on the Shotley peninsula, eight between the Orwell and Deben and eight between the Deben and Alde. The first Martello Towers were circular in plan with straight sides, but the design was gradually refined, and Suffolk towers were ovoid, to make their seaward side stronger, with sides tapering inwards to deflect cannon shot. The final tower, at Slaughden, near Aldeburgh, is England's northernmost and largest Martello Tower, with unique quatrefoil plan (standing on an exposed shingle beach, it was designed to be exceptionally strong). The towers contained a basement for storage and a first floor with living quarters for thirty men. Entrance was by a first-floor door, and many had a moat in case of landward assault. No tower ever experienced any military attack, and one on Orford Ness was lost to coastal erosion in 1822, but the other Suffolk towers remained in military preparedness until the 1870s and were used for coastal observation during the First and Second World Wars. Six more Suffolk towers have been lost to coastal erosion or modern development, but eleven survive. Two at Bawdsey (near some unusual military installations from the First and Second World Wars) are also threatened by coastal erosion, but in 2007 Suffolk County Council launched an initiative to fund coastal defences, ensuring their preservation for the immediate future.

No Suffolk Martello Towers are open to the public, but their exteriors can be seen.

Martello Tower near Langer Road, Felixstowe, adapted as a lookout point by the Customs Service.

Orford Ness

In 1913, the War Department acquired Orford Ness as a base for experimental flights. Paradoxically, whereas Orford Castle was built when Orford was a thriving seaport, the Ness was chosen for military research because the region had declined into a remote backwater, leaving it among the most inaccessible areas of the East Coast. During the First World War, parachutes, aerial photography and aeroplane gun and bomb sights, and the aeroplane camouflage paint NIVO Green (an acronym of 'Night Varnish Orfordness') were developed here. Sea walls and sluices were dug to drain and protect the site. Many were made by Chinese labourers and are still called 'Chinese Walls'; others were constructed by German prisoners-of-war.

Between 1935 and 1937, Robert Watson Watt ran the Ionospheric Research Station here, where he conducted the world's first experiments and demonstrations in the use of radar to monitor aeroplane activity, one of the most important episodes in the history of modern military technology. (He then moved his operations to Bawdsey, where they proved crucial to Britain's defence during the Second World War.) During the Second World War, further aviation experimentation took place, and allied and captured enemy planes were subjected to explosions and damage to test how they might function in combat or emergency. After this war AWRE (Atomic Weapons Research Establishment) Orfordness was established, to subject atomic weapon components to test drops, stress and pressure. Two huge concrete silos, built in 1966, officially called laboratories four and five but known as 'Pagodas', were used to subject Polaris Warhead components to test explosions. When this closed in 1971, the Cobra Mist Building was constructed by the US and UK governments at a cost of over £20 million. Part of a series of projects with the codename Cobra, developed to monitor Eastern Bloc military

The Black Beacon, a navigation beacon, with Orford Ness lighthouse in the background.

The 'Pagodas' on Orford Ness.

activity, it closed after only two years, supposedly because its signals suffered from interference (but possibly as a bargaining counter in the negotiation of international nuclear treaties). It is now the main transmitter for the BBC World Service Radio.

Restricted human access caused Orford Ness to become a significant nature reserve, and it is now managed by the National Trust and open to visitors. Access is by ferry only, but since the site is very large, visitors should wear strong footwear, allow plenty of time for exploration, and be aware of ferry departure times. It should also be emphasised that the Ness contains unexploded bombs, so visitors must carefully observe all warning notices. Contact the National Trust for admission details.

6

CHURCHES

No English county possesses a wider and finer selection of historic churches than Suffolk. In 1086 the *Domesday Book* recorded 448 churches here – more than the rest of England put together. From such a wealth of buildings, only a few examples can be discussed here.

Bury St Edmunds Cathedral

Medieval and modern spiritual traditions meet in St James's Church in Bury St Edmunds. Founded by Abbot Anselm of Bury after monastic duties prevented him making a pilgrimage to the shrine of St James at Compostella in Spain, it was rebuilt in the sixteenth century. St James's emblems of scallop shells and pilgrims' staves appear on the exterior west wall. Edward VI gave £200 to complete it, although, because of its late construction, it lacked a proper chancel.

In 1913, St James's was chosen as the cathedral for Suffolk as it was the only church in the county that could be enlarged without destroying medieval work, while its location by the Abbey Gardens gave space to extend it. Two world wars and the intervening Depression prevented the planned enlargements until the 1960s, when Stephen Dykes-Bower, the only architect who then upheld the Gothic tradition, designed a porch, south cloister walk, chancel and transepts in an updated Perpendicular style. In his will, Stephen Dykes-Bower left money to build a central tower. After further fund-raising, new work began under the Gothic Design Practice's direction, and the 160ft tower, a modern interpretation of the medieval vision, now forms a magnificent addition to the Bury skyline.

Polstead

At Polstead, bricks surround the twelfth-century chancel arch, nave arcade arches and clerestory window. Their dimensions and appearance are sufficiently distinct from Roman bricks to lead many experts to suggest that these are the earliest post-Roman bricks in England.

St James's Cathedral at Bury St Edmunds, showing the new tower. (Photograph by Ian Hulland, courtesy of St Edmundsbury Cathedral)

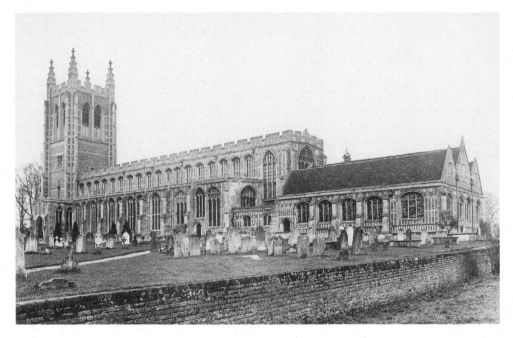

Long Melford Church.

Long Melford

The exterior battlements at Long Melford Church incorporate lengthy inscriptions naming the fifteenth-century clothiers who financed the building, especially the Cloptons of Kentwell Hall. Many donors are represented in an amazing series of stained-glass windows in the north aisle, among England's largest collections of medieval portraiture. A north-east chapel was a separate, freestanding building, but as the church grew, they were linked together. This chapel's roof displays a religious poem on panels stretching from God's hand, while the window incorporates an exquisite stained-glass portrayal of Jesus crucified on a lily. An eastern Lady Chapel is unique in being wholly separated from the rest of the church. (After the Reformation it became a school, when a multiplication table was painted on the wall.) Sir William Clopton's memorial is preserved from an earlier church. In 1436 he left Hadleigh Town Hall to the townspeople in return for an annual rent of a red rose, to be placed on his tomb, the longest continual rent paid in Britain.

The spectacular font cover at Ufford Church.

Ufford

Ufford Church contains a dramatic font cover, 18ft high, with a profusion of pinnacles and tabernacles springing from canopied niches. Henry Munro Cautley, an architect and a leading authority on Suffolk churches, described it as the most beautiful example of its kind in the world. A war memorial window shows a British solider and a sailor helping Jesus carry the cross.

Kedington

Kedington Church has been described as the 'Westminster Abbey of Suffolk' from its memorials to the Barnardiston family who converted from Roman Catholicism to Puritanism after the Reformation, becoming leading Parliamentarians during the Civil War. They reordered the church for Puritan worship, reconstructing a fifteenth-century screen as a family pew (probably in 1619, when the present chancel screen was erected) from where they could enjoy sermons delivered from the three-decker pulpit. (Unfortunately, an inappropriately sited organ behind the pulpit now spoils the view of the earliest Barnardiston monuments.) Schoolchildren sat on tiered seats at the end of the aisles; the pews before these faced backwards, so their teachers could watch them. A tenth-century stone cross head was found under the floor in 1860; it now stands before the east window – Suffolk's oldest altar.

S.S. Peter and Paul, Kedington, Three Decker Pulpit   PN5026

The three-decker pulpit at Kedington Church, with the Barnardiston's family pew in the background.

Walpole Old Chapel

Walpole Old Chapel is one of England's oldest nonconformist meeting houses. In 1649 a Congregational (or Independent) group formed in the area. Following the Act of Toleration in 1689, they adapted a house at Walpole for their meetings. It contains an austere, but unusually splendid interior, with a central three-decker pulpit and galleries around three sides. Differences between the construction of the galleries to the east and west suggest that the house was first converted into a chapel when Nonconformity was proscribed, and then enlarged when it received legal toleration.

Lound

When Booth Lines became vicar of the small church at Lound in 1908, he commissioned the artist-craftsman Ninian Comper to recreate the colourful interior of a medieval church. Ninian Comper painted and gilded the medieval rood screen with pictures of saints, topping it with an image of the crucified Christ (with serpents below to symbolise vanquished evil). He executed a wall painting of St Christopher, the patron saint of travellers, showing himself driving a car. (During restoration in 1964, an aeroplane was added.)

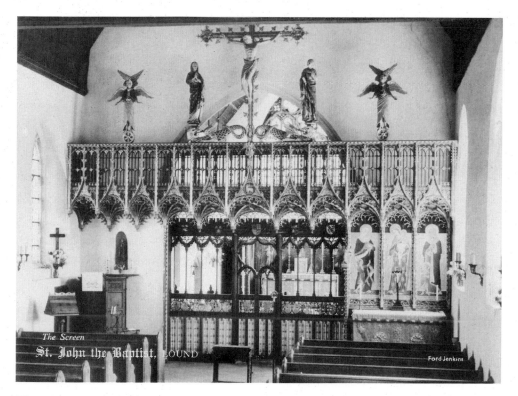

The screen at Lound Church.

Norfolk Horn ram in the east window at Herringswell.

Herringswell

Herringswell Church contains some of England's finest twentieth-century stained glass, and it might be fun to try to count all the Breckland birds and animals portrayed here. The east window shows Jesus as the good shepherd, flanked by sheep. The Davies family, who commissioned this, were sheep farmers, and the animals were taken from drawings of their flock of Norfolk Horn and Suffolk black-faced sheep, including a Norfolk Horn as the 'ram in the thicket' (Genesis 22:13). Another scene portrays Francis of Assisi holding a hare while scattering seed for birds. A window commemorating a field sports enthusiast shows one of his favourite springer spaniels, and glass by Ivona Mays-Smith, a local woman, shows Herringswell in spring, including her cocker spaniel, Tiffany. The visitors' book, although not large, begins in September 1945, and still has empty pages, the oldest continually used visitors' book I have seen in an extensive career of church-crawling; a double surprise, since the glass should attract visitors from all over the country.

Suffolk black-faced sheep in the east window at Herringswell.

Springer spaniel in the stained glass at Herringswell.

The east window at Herringswell Church.

Melton Chapel

After a Primitive Methodist chapel was built at Melton in 1860, the owner of the neighbouring house took the chapel trustees to court, claiming 'Ancient Lights', on the grounds that it blocked light to the side of his house. When the court found in his favour in 1861, the trustees had the chapel moved by cutting through the foundations, raising it on jacks, and carrying it 18ft on wooden rollers to its present location.

Window at Herringswell Church showing St Francis of Assisi.

Two Churches in One Churchyard

In some places two churches share one churchyard, as at Trimley, where St Mary's and St Martin's are 100yds apart. At Bungay, St Mary and Holy Trinity churchyards are nearly contiguous, although separated by Trinity Street. The Victorian Roman Catholic church of St Edmund was built on the south side of St Mary's churchyard. Although a wall separates them, it could be argued that Bungay contains three churches in adjoining churchyards. (St Mary's shared a churchyard with another church dedicated to St Thomas, which vanished after the Reformation.)

The Primitive Methodist chapel at Melton being moved. (From *The Illustrated London News* of 5 October 1861)

St Mary's Church and St Martin's Church at Trimley.

In 1904, Edward Cecil Guinness, the first Earl of Iveagh, commissioned the architect William Caroe to enlarge St Andrew's Church at Elveden to complement Elveden Hall. Caroe added a northern nave and chancel in a style described as 'Art Nouveau Gothic', to create one of England's most beautiful twentieth-century churches. The old and new churches of St Andrew and St Patrick (a nod to Lord Iveagh's Irish ancestry) retain their integrity in a remarkable way. The Earl also had a bell tower built in memory of his wife at the entrance to the Hall's grounds, joined to the church by a cloister-walk – the only church in Suffolk with two connected towers.

St James's Church and St Mary's Church at Bury St Edmunds were built on the perimeter of the abbey (and town) graveyard. Both extend beyond the abbey precincts; it has been theorised that this was so people could enter without asking the monks' permission.

At Pakefield, two churches, All Saints and St Margaret's share one building; they were separated by a wall until the parishes were united in 1746. It has been suggested that one replaced an earlier church lost to coastal erosion; alternatively, St Margaret's might have served Kirkley, a nearby hamlet (now merged into Lowestoft). Pakefield Church was hit by incendiary bombs in the Second World War but was restored and reopened in 1950: the first English church lost to war damage to be fully restored to worship.

Church Towers

Forty-one medieval Suffolk churches possess round towers. There are twelve in the Lothingland peninsula, the northernmost part of Suffolk between the North Sea and the River Waveney; others are scattered unevenly across the county. England's largest round church tower stands at Wortham; 29ft in diameter, it is now roofless. The narrowest stands

The interior of Pakefield Church, seen following its repair from war damage; the arcade dividing the building into two was not opened until the eighteenth century.

Wortham Church, with the largest round church tower in England.

Bundeston Church, with the narrowest round church tower in England.

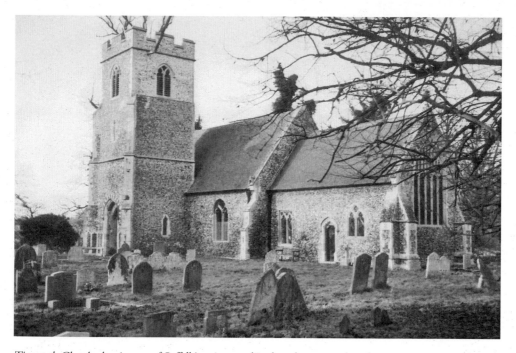

Timworth Church, showing one of Suffolk's unique combined south towers and porches.

at Blundeston, little more than 10ft in diameter. A round tower at Little Saxham displays Romanesque (or Norman) arcading; that at Ashby has a circular lower stage, but the top stages are octagonal, containing medieval bricks. At Wickham Market the tower is of similar construction, but octagonal from foundation to roof. At Barsham, the adjoining nave wall is covered with plaster, showing that it predates the tower. Evidently, round towers were built well into the Middle Ages.

Churches with south towers, the ground floors of which double as porches, are unique to Suffolk. There are twenty-six medieval examples in the county, of which twenty-two can be seen near the rivers Gipping and Deben in the south-east of the county. The largest and most impressive is St Mary-le-Tower in Ipswich (a Victorian rebuilding over a medieval original); other good examples can be seen at Grundisburgh, Haughley, Newbourne and Playford.

At Beccles the church was built by the valley of the River Waveney. This precluded a west tower. Instead, there is a 97ft-high detached tower to the south-east, overlooking the Market Place. In 1973, the parochial church council decided it was unable to maintain it, and sold it to Beccles Town Council for one penny (displayed on the tower wall) after which the Beccles Society raised £63,000 to restore it.

At East Bergholt, work on a tower stopped in 1530. Instead, the bells were hung in a wooden 'bell cage'; as they did not have to be taken up a tower, their combined weight is over four tons – England's heaviest five-bell peal. They point upwards, as they would be too heavy to move if hung downwards, and the ringers rock them.

Left: *The brass of Sir Robert de Bures at Acton Church, from a rubbing by the Revd Henry Tyrrell Green of Santon Downham.* (By courtesy of Acton P.C.C. and the Suffolk Institute of Archaeology)

Below: *John Baret's cadaver tomb in St Mary's Church in Bury St Edmunds.*

Monuments

Acton Church contains a memorial brass to Sir Robert de Bures, a soldier in Edward I's military campaigns. Installed in 1330, it is 6ft 6in long, and is often cited as the finest military brass in existence; it is also a candidate for the oldest memorial brass. Sir Robert's descendant, Henry Bures, the last of the line, also appears on a brass in the armour of Henry VIII's reign.

Henry VIII's sister, Mary Tudor, is buried in St Mary's Church in Bury St Edmunds. She married King Louis XII of France; after his death, she married Charles Brandon, the Duke of Suffolk. She was interred in a plain tomb chest in Bury Abbey; after the Dissolution, this was moved to the chancel of St Mary's. She was re-interred below the floor in 1784, under the top of her tomb. John Baret, a fifteenth-century merchant, had the east bay of the south aisle at St Mary's converted into a chantry, where masses could be held for his soul. Roof decorations incorporate mirror glass (very expensive at that time). John Baret is commemorated by a 'cadaver' tomb, showing an emaciated dead body. Medical opinion holds that it is anatomically accurate; possibly it was copied from an actual corpse. Another cadaver tomb at Denston shows John and Katherine Denston as emaciated corpses wrapped in shrouds.

William Phelip, Baron Bardolph, a veteran of Agincourt, a knight of the Garter and Treasurer to Henry VI, converted the east bay of the south aisle of Dennington into a chantry, placing his memorial with coloured alabaster effigies of himself and his wife in the centre. Contemporary screenwork surrounds the memorial, while the ceiling is painted with stars. Wingfield contains some of England's most beautiful memorial effigies, including that of John De La Pole, the Duke of Suffolk and his wife, Elizabeth Plantagenet, the sister of Edward IV and Richard III.

At Framlingham, Thomas Howard, the third Duke of Norfolk, is buried in a monument displaying Renaissance sculpture of quality as high as any undertaken in Europe at the time.

FRAMLINGHAM CHURCH, (showing tombs.)

The spectacular tomb of Thomas Howard, third Duke of Norfolk, in Framlingham Church. The small alcove in the background is the tomb of an infant daughter of the Howard family. The tomb of Henry Howard, 'the poet Earl', stands to the far left.

His monument contains three bodies; it has been wondered if his grandfather and father, the first and second Dukes, who were buried at Thetford Priory in Norfolk, were removed here for reburial after the Dissolution. The third Duke's son, Henry Howard, Earl of Surrey, a leading poet, was executed because of Tudor court intrigue. The political climate was such that his stunning coloured alabaster monument was only erected seventy years after his death. A small recess in the wall marks the tomb of Elizabeth, the fourth Duke's daughter, who died in infancy.

Hengrave Hall was built in Henry VIII's reign for Thomas Kytson, a wealthy merchant. He predeceased his wife, Margaret, who remarried the Earl of Bath. A memorial in Hengrave Church shows Margaret and her noble husband on the tomb-chest, while Kytson, a mere tradesman, was placed in an alcove underneath, on the floor.

At Sudbourne, Sir Michael Stanhope's Jacobean memorial fills most of the chancel wall. The insription says: 'He sat at the feet of Elizabeth I for twenty years'. Evidently he was keen to be remembered: it also says that 'mindful of mortalitie, while he lived he erected this monument'. Great Saxham Church contains a coloured bust and an elaborate floor brass showing John Eldred, an Elizabethan merchant, who spent eight years travelling the Middle East. At Dalham, overlooking the altar, there is a wall memorial to Martin Stuteville, who sailed to America with Francis Drake. In Rushbrooke a poignant memorial describes how Thomas Jermyn, the last of his line, died aged fifteen on a ship when the mast fell on him. A small plaque on the south wall of Boxford records how Elizabeth Hyam, widowed four times, died in 1748, aged 113. In Halesworth, Andrew Johnston, a lieutenant in the Royal Flying Corps (the predecessor of the R.A.F.), is commemorated by a cross made from an aeroplane propeller.

Discoveries

Some unusual discoveries have been made in churches, sometimes proving long-standing traditions. Henry VIII's second wife, Anne Boleyn, was related to the Parker family of Erwarton. A story said she wished for her heart to be buried there. In 1836, a small, heart-shaped casket was found in the south wall of Erwarton Church: was Anne's wish fulfilled? During recent restoration, a 'heart shrine' was found in the south transept of Exning Church, a recess containing two sculpted pairs of hands, clasped in prayer over hearts. The identity of the people to whom this was raised has been forgotten.

In 1892, the whitewashed wooden panels were removed from the chancel arch at Wenhaston and thrown into the churchyard, to be burned the next day. By the most amazing good fortune, it rained that night, removing the whitewash to reveal an early sixteenth-century painting of the Last Judgement. This must have been painted over at the Reformation. A rare example of late-medieval artwork, it is now preserved in the church.

An eighteenth-century squire left his library to Brent Eleigh Church. The indefatigable scholar M.R. James found several medieval manuscripts here, including illuminated gospels once owned by St Margaret of Scotland. Realisation of their value led to their transfer to Oxford and Cambridge Universities. After this, the printed books were dispersed and the library building fell down. But the discovery inspired M.R. James to write his first ghost story, *Canon Alberic's Scrapbook*.

In 1878, a box containing 2,600 twelfth- and thirteenth-century silver pennies was found under the floor of Sudbourne Church. We can only speculate on why they were hidden here and then forgotten for six centuries.

St Botolph's Church at Iken overlooks the Alde estuary. Botolph was a seventh-century abbot who founded a famous monastery at a place called Icanho. There was no certain proof that this was Iken. But, after a fire destroyed the church's thatched roof, Stanley West, the county archaeologist, discovered a tenth-century carved stone cross shaft in the tower arch. It was proposed that the cross was made in Botolph's honour, suggesting that Iken Church indeed stood on the site of his monastery.

Wall Paintings

In the Middle Ages, the interior walls of English churches were decorated with religious paintings. Few of these survive, but Suffolk contains some exceptional examples. Wissington's lovely Norman church contains a thirteenth-century representation of St Francis of Assisi preaching to the birds – the earliest known representation of this beautiful subject – and an incredible animated dragon. At Hessett, personifications of the seven deadly sins rise from a tree from the mouth of hell, above a representation of 'Christ of the Trades', showing Jesus surrounded by tools. These include a six of diamonds, the earliest picture of a playing card. Paintings at North Cove, showing the story of the crucifixion, have recently been conserved,

Wall painting at Wissington of St Francis of Asissi preaching to the birds. (From a drawing by Hamlet Watling)

Wall painting of St Walstan of Bawburgh at Cavenham.

leading to the uncovering of new details, including a portrayal of the donor who paid for the work.

Sometimes wall paintings are found under modern plaster or furniture. A fourteenth-century representation of the crucifixion was found on the east wall at Brent Eleigh – the oldest English medieval altar painting in its original location. At Ilketshall St Andrew, several excellent pictures, including a Wheel of Fortune have just been discovered and meticulously conserved. A small painting of a man with a crown and a scythe was found in Cavenham; this has been identified as St Walstan of Bawburgh, a legendary Norfolk prince who became a farm worker. Badly affected by damp, it urgently requires conservation if it is not to be lost forever.

Ruined Churches

There is an unresolved debate as to whether the ruined church called South Elmham Minster was an Anglo-Saxon cathedral. A cathedral was established at a place called Elmham in 673, and moved to Norwich in 1095, but it is unclear if it was here, or at North Elmham in Norfolk, where there is another ruined church. Carved stone, thought to date from the tenth century, had been re-used in the Minster's foundations, establishing the earliest possible building date. But Herbert de Losinga, the first Bishop of Norwich, built a residence at South Elmham, leaving the possibility that it was a Norman bishop's chapel. Even if the latter supposition is correct, was the Minster, which stands in an unusually remote location, built on the site of an earlier sacred building?

Bury St Edmunds Abbey Church was 485ft long, with a west front 245ft wide and a west tower at least 200ft high – the most complicated and ambitious west front of any church in Europe (longer and higher than the nearby St James's Cathedral). Describing its loss after the Dissolution would be too depressing, but the west front was too strongly built to be totally destroyed, and by the seventeenth century, houses had been built into the ruins, whose antiquarian atmosphere ensures that they remain desirable residences: a unique renewal of any British ruin.

A church was built at Orford at the same time as the castle. After the nave was rebuilt in the fourteenth century, the chancel was abandoned, but the ruined chancel arcades stand in the churchyard. In the fifteenth century, Walberswick was a thriving seafaring community, and a great new church was built to demonstrate its wealth. Walberswick later declined; the parishioners could only maintain the porch, south aisle and tower, but forsook the rest of the building, which now stands in ruin. After the Reformation, St Peter's Church at Eriswell was deserted and the ruins of the nave were converted into a dovecot.

The ruins of South Elmham Minster.

The ruins of the west front of Bury St Edmunds Abbey Church.

Walberswick Church.

Where the Wild Things Are

Many representations of animals and fantastic creatures appear in Suffolk churches. A figure on a pew in Dennington Church was something of a mystery, until M.R. James, when aged only fifteen, identified it as a sciapod. Medieval myth said that sciapods were people with one leg and one large foot, who lived in the tropics, and slept lying on their backs, each covering themselves with their foot.

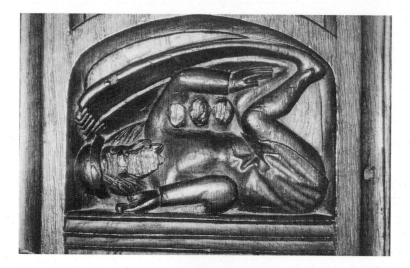

Above: *The Dennington sciapod.*

Right: *Glass roundel at Long Meford. Three hares sharing three ears symbolise the Trinity.*

At Bramford an extraordinary array of stone creatures on the battlements outside the north nave and aisle roof include a bear, and a monkey examining a urine flask – a popular medieval satire of the doctors of the time. Another row of animals sits above the battlements on the south of Blythburgh, including another monkey, this time wearing a monk's robe.

St Nicholas's Church in Ipswich contains two twelfth-century sculptures believed to come from lost medieval churches in the town. One shows a wild boar, with a prominent snout and tusks. The other shows an angel fighting a dragon with a coiled tail, with an Old English inscription which can be translated as: 'Here St Michael fought the dragon'. Both carvings show strong Viking influence. St Peter's in Ipswich possesses a twelfth-century black Tournai marble font, with twelve stylised lions on the bowl.

The door at Wordwell Church contains a twelfth-century tympanum showing two animals, possibly dogs or lions, standing beside the tree of life, entwined in the foliage; a motif whose origins have been traced to Iraq in the seventh century BC.

A small glass roundel in the north aisle at Long Melford shows three hares' heads, connected by the ears, so that while there are only three ears in the image, each hare still has two ears. This device, which originated in the Far East in the thirteenth century, was used to represent the Trinity.

The north aisle roof at Mildenhall Church.

At Mildenhall, a long row of swans float along the cornice of the south aisle roof, while lions and dragons peer down from the north aisle roof beams. Wooden carvings of horses, deer and lions run along the roof cornices at Denston, while a misericord in the choir shows a crane standing on one foot and holding a stone in the other. Medieval legend said that when a flock of cranes went to sleep, one stayed awake to mount guard, holding a stone in its talons so that if it, too, fell asleep, the noise of the falling stone would wake it.

Above the south door outside Santon Downham, there is a twelfth-century carving of a lion with a foliage tail. Inside the church a modern window shows Francis of Assisi surrounded by Breckland birds, avoiding sentimentality by showing an owl carrying a mouse (my nomination for Suffolk's finest example of modern stained glass).

Claydon Church was extensively rebuilt by Father George Drury, a Victorian rector; much of the decoration was his own handiwork. Corbels (roof supports) in the chancel display carvings of lavish foliage. It is possible that Father George wished to remind people of the Garden of Eden, for the north-west corbel shows a serpent entwined in the vegetation.

A small, often overlooked feature in St James's Cathedral in Bury is a carved stone mouse on the base of the pulpit. At St Peter's Church in Sudbury, four griffins stand guard at the corner of the tower. It was decided to frighten pigeons from the tower roof by placing a plastic owl on the battlements. Overlooking Market Hill, it is remarkably convincing: people have watched it wondering why it doesn't move.

In 1904, stained-glass representations of green dragons were found under the floor at Barton Mills Church. These fitted neatly into the upper tracery of several nave windows, and the building is sometimes called 'the church of the green dragon'.

Bench end carvings exercised medieval craftsmen's minds. At Stowlangtoft there is a mermaid, a bear and two unicorns; at Ixworth Thorpe there is a mermaid and a unicorn; at Lakenheath there is a whale. More unicorns can be seen at Honington and Tostock, and another mermaid at Dennington. There are two monkeys at Woolpit, one dressed as a monk. At Wortham a Victorian bench ends to illustrate Psalm 104: look out for the sea serpent!

Lion with foliate tail at Santon Downham.

A true pride of lions keep watch at the west door of Stoke-By-Nayland Church; while four stand on guard on the lintels, fourteen lion faces peer from the surround.

The wild man or *wodewose* was a popular figure in medieval iconography. A shaggy man with a long beard, covered from head to foot in hair, often carrying a club, he appears by the porch doors at Badingham, Cratfield, Ufford and Yaxley, and on the tower at Haverhill (as well as the battlements at Bramford). Sometimes he appears with lions; at Mendlesham two wild men and two rather rustic lions stand on the top of the north porch. Some east Suffolk fonts display lions and wild men around the bases. There are good examples at Halesworth, Haughley, St Clement's in Ipswich, Orford, Redlingfield and Saxmundham. Perhaps they were guardian figures, although they may not always have been friends: a misericord at Norton shows a lion eating a wild man.

Window at Santon Downham showing St Francis of Assisi surrounded by Breckland birds.

St Gregory's Church at Sudbury was extensively rebuilt in 1365, under the influence of Simon Theobald (alias Simon of Sudbury), a local clergyman who became Archbishop of Canterbury. The north aisle displays gargoyles and three roof bosses made from terracotta. The earliest terracotta sculpture in England, one roof boss displays a popular medieval figure: the Green Man. A ferocious foliage-covered face, sometimes with vegetation springing from his mouth, he may symbolise nature, order and disorder, a guardian spirit or mankind's primeval nature.

Other representations of the Green Man can be seen over the outer door of the porches at Woolpit and St Peter's in Sudbury; at Nayland he looks down from roof bosses on the the centre of the south-west porch and the nave roof west of the pulpit; at Bramford he appears at the apex of the tower arch; at Tostock he stares from the north side of the font. Stained-glass

Bend end carving of a sea serpent at Wortham.

representations appear in the upper lights of the north-west aisle window at Long Melford, the east window at Denston and a south chancel window at Woolpit. A foliate head over the nave doorway in the porch of Clare Church should be studied carefully. The outline of the face and features are distinctly feminine: this is a Green Woman. For an exceptional representation of Green Men, one should study the frieze along the top of the exterior of the south aisle at Acton Church. There are over ten representations, but every time I count them, I find a different total.

While at Acton, also look out for the dinosaurs. When the local history society staged an exhibition in the church, two model pterodactyls were placed under the north aisle roof and they were deliberately left there after the exhibition finished. But I hope they do not give you the same nasty shock they did me when I first saw them!

Green Woman at Clare.

Lion and wodewose (wildman) on a misericord at Norton.

Angel on the roof at St Mary's Church, Bury St Edmunds.

Huntingfield's incredible Victorian roof.

Angel Roofs

Angel roofs are outstanding features of some churches, and Suffolk possesses the highest concentration of such roofs in England. Wooden angels are carved on the roof beams at Bildeston, Little Whelnetham, Grundisburgh, Hawstead and Lakenheath, and spectacular displays soar on the roofs at Badingham, Earl Stonham, Woolpit and St Mary's in Bury. At Southwold angels in bright robes soar under a brilliant blue and gold roof. An angel at Bardwell holds a book with the date 1421, when Sir William de Bardwell (who appears in stained glass below), commissioned the roof. At Rattlesden, twentieth-century craftsmen restored the roof to incorporate a breathtaking heavenly host. But for an incredible re-modelling of a medieval roof, it would be impossible to match Huntingfield, often called 'Suffolk's Sistine Chapel'. Between 1859 and 1866, Mildred Holland, the rector's wife, repainted the roof. Working unassisted, she covered every inch with dazzling paintings to create a glorious pageant of colour that is sufficient to make one revise one's opinion of Victorian art.

This chapter has only sketched a very small proportion of the fantastic riches contained in Suffolk churches. In 1982, the Suffolk Historic Churches Trust initiated a new way to enjoy them by organising a sponsored cycle ride, the idea being for people to visit as many churches in the county as possible, either by bicycle or on foot, with people sponsoring them for each church they can visit within the day. Each participating walker or cyclist gives half the money they raise to a church of their choice and half to the Trust to help preserve the county's churches. The ride has been repeated every year since, on the second Saturday in September, raising over £6 million to help preserve Suffolk churches. The idea has been taken up by church preservation and appreciation societies in other counties. No sponsored event can offer a better opportunity to enjoy Suffolk's wonderful ecclesiastical heritage.

7

FOLLIES, GARDEN LODGES AND MAZES

Follies are buildings designed to embellish the landscape, rather than serve an obviously practical function. The word 'folly' implies an extravagance or waste of money, something that is unnecessarily expensive. Architectural follies were obviously built at some cost, and some seem to be of limited practical value or display a disproportionate amount of ornaments. Nevertheless, they provide intangible benefits, for how can you quantify the benefits of a beautiful landscape or garden?

Freston Tower

Freston Tower is a six-storey red brick structure by the shores of the Orwell; each storey contains one room, connected by a spiral staircase in a corner turret which continues to the roof for a spectacular view of the Orwell estuary. It cannot have served a military purpose as its many windows would make it difficult to defend; it is unnecessarily elaborate for a watchtower, and does not appear to have possessed any practical function (it contains no hearths or fireplaces). It has therefore been suggested that this was England's first 'folly'.

In 1843 Richard Cobbold, the author of *Margaret Catchpole*, wrote *Freston Tower*, a historical romance based around an imagined history of the building, which claimed that it was built for the education of Ellen de Freston, who studied a different subject in each room for six days of the week and on the roof on the seventh (one must hope that Ellen was a hardy child if she had to study on an open rooftop or in rooms without fireplaces). Ellen de Freston was an imaginary character, yet this wholly fictional story has found its way into many books, to confuse many papers on the tower's history. Dendrochronology of selected timbers now suggests a building date of 1578 or 1579. Thomas Gooding, an Ipswich merchant, bought the manor of Freston in 1554. He was granted the right to bear arms in 1576, so it seems plausible that he had the tower built to celebrate his rise to fortune.

One Clare Hunt acquired Freston Tower as a holiday home, and gave it to the Landmark Trust, so 'lots of people can enjoy a building where I have been very happy'. It is now an upmarket holiday home (modern central heating and sanitation have been installed).

Freston Tower.

The Tattingstone Wonder

The Tattingstone Wonder is the county's most famous folly, featuring in more studies of these buildings than any other in Suffolk. In about 1790, Edward White of Tattingstone Place adapted two existing cottages by adding a third, which was topped with a façade tower, lacking a south wall. Pointed Gothic windows were inserted into the cottages' north and east walls, but conventional doors and windows were retained to the south and west, so that while the building looks like a church from Tattingstone Place, it still appears as a row of cottages from the main road. One of its functions was to serve as an eye-catcher, making an attractive focal point in the view from Tattingstone Place. Tradition avers that the name derives from Edward White's statement that since people wondered at nothing, he would give them something to wonder at.

The Tattingstone Wonder.

Banqueting House at Euston Park.

Garden Follies

Most follies were built to adorn parks surrounding country mansions. A watermill at Euston Hall had a tower attached so it would resemble a church, creating an eye-catcher from Euston Hall. In his diary, John Evelyn observed that the river at Euston had been canalised, terminating in a cascade that powered a watermill and a pump to supply water to the Hall and garden. Replacement milling machinery was made by Burrell's engineering works at Thetford (a famous manufacturer of traction engines), the only such apparatus this company made. The mill can be visited when Euston Hall is open to visitors during the summer. In the eighteenth century, the second Duke of Grafton commissioned William Kent to rebuild Euston Hall, but the only part of his design to be constructed was a banqueting house, whose Palladian appearance led it to be called the Temple. The third and fourth Dukes used it to watch their horses being exercised. Now a private house, its exterior can be seen from the park.

While Redgrave Hall has been demolished and much of the grounds turned over to agriculture, a garden folly known as the Temple or Round House survives. A windowless, octagonal building with a domed roof, it has been identified as the work of 'Capability' Brown, who worked at Redgrave, although it is possible that it was designed rather later by an unidentified architect. Now privately owned, and not open to the public, it can be seen from the main road.

Great Saxham Hall, an Elizabethan mansion, burnt down in 1779. Hutchinson Mure, the then owner, an amateur inventor and scientist, designed an elaborate new house in a fashionable classical style and landscaped a park around it, including two follies: the larger, originally called the 'Temple of Dido', but later named 'Grandfather's', is a two-storey hexagonal building with three porches, ornamented with rusticated stonework. It may have been part of the estate farm, or an estate worker's house. A smaller folly, of similar, but

The Tea House at Great Saxham.

more modest design, contains one room. Originally called the 'Temple in the Shrubbery', in Victorian times windows were inserted and a pointed roof was added to turn it into a little Tea House (its present name). Hutchinson Mure went bankrupt (partly because of his elaborate building schemes) and Great Saxham Hall was sold to Thomas Mills, who was probably responsible for a third folly, the 'Umbrello', at the end of a walk at the furthest end of the grounds. A Neo-Gothic octagonal canopy, made of white Coade Stone, it has been suggested that it was meant to provide a view of Ickworth House. 'Grandfather's' is a private house, but can be seen from the road south of the church. The grounds of Great Saxham Hall are open on the first Sunday of April for the Red Cross Open Gardens Scheme, when the other two follies can be seen.

The 'Leaning Tower of Eye', a small octagonal garden lodge for a house in Magdalen Street, was built in 1812 and given a castellated appearance with battlements around the top. Left to

The Leaning Tower of Eye.

deteriorate for many years, the lean was caused when tree roots spread under the foundations, but it was restored by Gerald Faulkner, the present owner. Although strictly private, it can be seen from the garden gate.

When the Henniker family financed a restoration of Thornham Magna Church, fragments of the old church were reassembled as a garden lodge for Thornham Park. Called the 'Hermitage', it resembled a little chapel, and contained a fireplace so it could be used in winter. It fell into ruin, but the Henniker family have recently restored it. Renamed the 'Folly', it is accessible when Thornham Walks are open to the public.

When the Revd George Drury rebuilt Claydon Church in 1862, he reused material from the medieval church to build a walled garden in the rectory grounds. A symbolic recreation of Jerusalem, it features two towers, one of which was meant to be the house of the Last Supper. Although privately owned, the exterior can be seen from Claydon churchyard.

The Folly at
Thornham Walks.

Erwarton Hall with its unusual gatehouse.

Gatehouses

Erwarton Hall is an exceptionally attractive privately owned Elizabethan house. An ornamental gatehouse in front of the garden could be classified as a folly, for it is covered with round gables and pillars. There is no clear evidence for its building date, although the seventeenth century seems most plausible.

Rendlesham Hall has been demolished, but two spectacular folly gatehouses survive. Nikolaus Pevsner wrote: '. . . and may they long survive; for they are the most memorable follies of Suffolk!' They were probably built for Peter Thelluson at the start of the nineteenth century, possibly when he was created Baron Rendlesham (thus showing the symbolic power of the gatehouse in defining the owner's status). Ivy Lodge is a ruined Gothic arch with flanking towers, the larger of which contains a gatekeeper's house. Both towers are capped with hollow open chambers to enhance the appearance of a ruin. Woodbridge Lodge, a hexagonal building surmounted by pinnacles and flying buttresses, is, for its size, as elaborate a piece of neo-Gothic architecture as any in England. Apparently copied from the Market Cross at Chichester, in some ways the design is even more elaborate. A new owner has recently saved it from dereliction, and is restoring it as a country residence (flanking it with a quite unconventional semi-circular house).

Edwardstone Hall, a Victorian building on the site of an earlier manor house, has also been demolished, but the gateway to the hall grounds survives (also guarding the approach to the parish church). Known locally as the 'Bar', it is a large redbrick arch covering the road, flanked by a Tudor Gothic-style tower.

Woodbridge Lodge, Rendlesham.

Ivy Lodge, Rendlesham.

Bramfield Folly.

Castles and Towers

Some follies have been built in the form of castles to recreate the appearance of history and archaeology; people may even have thought it amusing to live in a building that resembled a castle. St Andrew's Castle in Bury St Edmunds was built in a whimsical Gothic style, with a castellated boundary wall against St Andrew's Street, from which it derives its present name. First appearing on a town map in 1791, it was once known as 'Sparkes' Castle', suggesting that it was built for Ezekiel Sparkes, a Bury solicitor of the time. It later became the home of the Boby family, who established an engineering business nearby, and then a convent school, before becoming a business centre.

Broad House at Oulton stands on a promontory overlooking Oulton Broad. Once part of a local estate, it was remodelled in a castellated Gothic style in the eighteenth century. Later the house of Nicholas Everitt, a sportsman and author, it now houses the Lowestoft Museum.

Bramfield Folly, a late eighteenth-century farmhouse built in a romantic castellated style, stands north-east of the church. Possibly intended as an eye-catcher for Bramfield Hall, it can be seen to its best advantage from Bramfield churchyard. Castle Farm at Worlingham, a farmhouse built to resemble a Norman castle, was probably designed by Francis Sandys, the architect of Ickworth, while working on Worlingham Hall, possibly as an 'eyecatcher' from the Hall.

The castle in St John's Street in Woodbrige, an attempt to recreate an urban building as a castle, with a side tower and a stucco frontage incorporating castellated decorations, was built as a club for army officers stationed here during the Napoleonic Wars.

Sir Edward Kerrison, a veteran of the Napoleonic Wars, had a modern keep, about 15ft high, built on the castle mound at Eye. A remarkably convincing antiquarian folly, it contained a retirement home for Edward Kerrison's batman (personal servant) who served him at

Folly tower at the Red House in Sudbury.

Waterloo. It seems most appropriate that a Victorian castle should have been built as a home for an old soldier, although we must hope he had no difficulty ascending and descending the mound! The house fell down in the twentieth century, so the sham ruin became a real ruin. Eye Castle was recently excavated by the Suffolk Archaeological Unit and turned into a public park.

Bungay is known for its ruined castle. Another ruin overlooking the Waveney is not so well known. John Barber Scott, the Bungay diarist and author, built a folly ruin in his garden at Bridge House, using material from the ruined nunnery attached to St Mary's Church (parts of which were being demolished). On 3 June 1841, John wrote in his diary: 'finish my ruins in Bridge House garden which have given me employment and amusement for the last two years.' He enjoyed it when visitors thought the ruins were genuinely medieval. Although Bridge House is privately owned, the ruins' exterior can be inspected from a footpath adjoining Castle Lane.

There are three folly towers at Sudbury, two stories high, with exterior surfaces decorated with a patchwork of red bricks and coloured stones and rocks. Thought to have been built in about 1840, the identity of the architect or craftsman who created them is a mystery. One, at the top of Constitution Hill, may have been part of a garden that has been eroded by suburban development; its walls and doors are bricked up and the surface has deteriorated badly. The second stands in Belle Vue Park. Built as a garden ornament for Ingram's Well House, the walls and doors have been blocked for public safety. The third stands in the gardens of the Red House, at the corner of Meadow Lane and Bullock's Lane. The Red House, one of Sudbury's most impressive Georgian houses, is now a private nursing home, but the tower can be seen over the wall or through the garden gates; the walls and doors are still open, although the interior is derelict. A stone summer house with an arcaded front in the gardens of a Stour Street house was clearly built by the same craftsman. Adrian Bell moved to Sudbury with his family in 1929 and adopted this as a study, from where he wrote an autobiographical novel, *Corduroy*. Bell became a successful novelist; also a crossword enthusiast, he devised the first ever *Times* crossword from his Sudbury summer house. This building clearly deserves to be regarded as a literary shrine among follies! Although private property, and not accessible to the public, the roof and battlements can be seen from Stour Street car park.

Banqueting Houses

Banqueting houses were popular adjuncts of Elizabethan and Stuart houses. A banquet, in this context, was the final course of a social meal, which people enjoyed while admiring the garden and watching the people outside. Seckford Hall was built for Sir Thomas Seckford, in the parish of Great Bealings on the periphery of Woodbridge. A banqueting house, known as the 'Gazebo', stands near Seckford Hall, on the edge of a walled garden, overlooking the approach road to Woodbridge. It straddles a steep slope, so that while its external face is only two stories high, its garden façade is four stories high. Now a private house, its exterior can be seen.

The beautiful octagonal banqueting house at Long Melford Hall was built at the start of the seventeenth century. In the eighteenth century, new windows were inserted and a heater installed in the basement, possibly to convert it into an orangery. Long Melford Hall is now a National Trust property and the banqueting house can be visited when the Hall is open .

The banqueting house at Long Melford (now a National Trust property).

Fishing Lodges

An Elizabethan fishing lodge at the corner of the moat surrounding Denham Hall (near Barrow in West Suffolk) conveys a feeling of Elizabethan sportsmanship. It was built for Edward Lewkenor, who ran Denham Hall as a puritan religious academy. One of the more appealing members of the puritan elite, who arranged communal meals for villagers at his house, he and his family kneel in prayer in a large memorial in the nearby parish church. Denham Hall is a private house, but the fishing lodge can be seen from a public footpath running alongside the moat.

The Museum of East Anglian Life at Stowmarket stands within the grounds of Abbots Hall, so named as it was a manor of the abbots of Bury. Behind the Hall there are two fishponds, the larger of which contains a rectangular island, topped by a small eighteenth-century rectangular red brick fishing lodge.

Gardens with Mazes

Sir Morton Peto, the developer of Lowestoft, bought Somerleyton Hall in 1843 and had it rebuilt in an extravagant Jacobean style. He commissioned the elaborate gardens, which include a large hedge maze with a central mound, topped by a chinoiserie pagoda. The maze can be explored when Somerleyton Hall is open to visitors during the summer.

Kentwell Hall, at Long Melford, is approached by an avenue of lime trees, ¾ mile long, planted in 1678, while both the hall and the gardens are surrounded by interconnected moats. A Victorian gazebo at a corner of the moat has been turned into a 'camera obscura', giving views of the grounds. In 1985, a pavement maze in the form of a Tudor rose was laid out in

Abbots Hall fishing lodge at the Museum of East Anglian Life at Stowmarket.

The maze at Somerleyton Hall.

the courtyard in front of the Hall to celebrate the 500th anniversary of the Tudor dynasty's accession to the throne. Made from 26,000 bricks, it can be walked as a unicursal maze (with one continuous passage) or six puzzle mazes.

The gardens at Shrubland Park, near Coddenham, were designed by Charles Barry, the architect of the Houses of Parliament. They feature the 'Descent', an incredible Italianate stairway rising up a hillside, an accurate replica of a Swiss chalet in an alpine garden, and an unusually difficult hedge maze. (Shrubland has recently changed hands, and it is uncertain if the gardens will be opened to the public.)

The Oakes family, Bury St Edmunds bankers, lived at Nowton Court. When the south porch of St Mary's Church in Bury was removed during road widening, they had it rebuilt in Nowton Park as a folly ruin. St Edmundsbury Borough Council now runs Nowton Park as a public amenity. A storm-damaged western red cedar was dying. Native Americans made totem poles from these trees, so instead of it being cut down, it was carved it into a totem pole, showing a grizzly bear, a raven, a man and a white wolf holding St Edmund's head between its forepaws. A puzzle maze was planted nearby in 1992 in the outline of a stylised oak tree (for the Oakes family) with 2,500 hornbeams forming 2 miles of hedging.

Two modern mazes can be explored at Haverhill. One was laid out in coloured stone on Peas Hill, the former market place; as at Kentwell, it can be explored as a unicursal labyrinth or several puzzle mazes. The 'Millennium Maze' in Haverhill's East Town Park is a series of mounds and willow-lined passages. A labyrinth (or single path maze) with a decorative sundial in the centre was recently laid out on the grass in an open space beside Church Road in Elmswell.

8

LOST VILLAGES AND TOWNS

S ome villages and towns which might once have been communities of importance have disappeared or shrunk into insignificance, but these can leave evocative traces of human activity.

Wordwell

Wordwell appeared in the *Domesday Book* as a village of eighteen families, suggesting a population of 100, but the Poll Tax of 1377 showed only nineteen adults. It is hard to avoid the conclusion that Wordwell was decimated by the Black Death. Standing on the edge of the Breckland, it was given over to sheep farming. By the eighteenth century, the only standing buildings were the church, one of the smallest in Suffolk, the manor farmhouse and a shepherd's hut.

Buxlow

Buxlow was a parish with its own church, yet there were fewer than ten houses there in 1428. Too small to continue as a viable community, it simply dwindled away. In 1650, the church was described as 'decayed and ruinated time out of mind', and the parish was later consolidated with Knodishall. The former village green is still a public open space. The Hall, rebuilt in the seventeenth century, is a farmhouse, and the ruins of the church tower stand in a garden.

Empakred Villages

Some villages have been removed to make way for country mansions and their parks. The Hervey family were Lords of the Manor of Ickworth from the fifteenth century; John Hervey, who was created Earl of Bristol in 1714, had much of the parish turned into a park, in preparation for the construction of a new mansion. But he had ten children, many of whom proved spendthrifts. Maintaining them reduced his aspirations, so his country seat was never built, although his grandson, the Earl Bishop, would build a truly memorable mansion here.

Wordwell Hall, north-west of the parish church, showing part of the site of the lost village.

The ruins of Buxlow Church.

The Mere at Livermere, showing the denuded village of Little Livermere.

Village settlements stood north-west of the parish church, and near Ickworth Lodge, north-west of the Earl Bishop's stately home. The medieval parish church, south of the mansion, is now neglected and shockingly being allowed to decay. Uneven bumps and hollows within the park remain to show the village's lost roads, paths and agricultural systems.

Little Fakenham was once called Great Fakenham, to distinguish it from the first Little Fakenham, a smaller adjoining village. In the seventeenth century, this was cleared away to make way for Euston Park; even the church was levelled. In the nineteenth century, the surviving village of Great Fakenham was renamed Little Fakenham to distinguish it from the Norfolk town with the same name.

In the eighteenth century, the Lee family became Lords of the Manors of Great and Little Livermere. Subsequently winning £30,000 in a state lottery, they landscaped a park around the lake which gave Livermere its name. This involved the removal of much of Little Livermere, although the church was kept and remodelled in a Gothic style, with a false top storey being added to the tower to make a more pleasing view from the Hall. After Livermere Hall was demolished in 1923, much of the park was turned over to agriculture. Little Livermere Church was tragically dismantled in 1948 and allowed to fall into ruin, although the central lake survives.

The 'three Fornhams'– Fornham All Saints, St Martin and St Genevieve, were the setting for a battle during a rebellion against Henry II's rule in 1173. A rebel army commanded by the Earl of Leicester was marching to the Midlands when royal forces, commanded by Robert de Lucy, blocked their route at the River Lark. The battle focused on the Sheepwash Bridge, a river crossing between Fornham All Saints and St Genevieve. The rebel army was overcome

The ruins of Fornham St Genevieve Church.

and the Earl taken prisoner. Tradition holds that some rebels made a 'last stand' at Fornham St Genevieve Church; more likely they fled there for sanctuary.

The Kent family, London merchants, built a mansion at Fornham St Genevieve. On 17 May 1775, a man was shooting at rooks on the church roof with a flintlock pistol when a spark ignited the thatch, and the church burnt down. (Accounts are unclear as to whether he was on the ground firing at birds on the roof, or on the roof firing at birds in the air.) The Kents used this as an excuse to remove the village to create a park. The Hall and park were used by the army during the Second World War, after which they fell into decay. A few years later, most of the Hall was demolished and large areas of the park were given over to gravel extraction and sewage disposal. Fornham St Genevieve is now closed, remote, barricaded and forlorn, but a small wood beside the River Lark has been opened as an enjoyable public amenity.

As a rule, villages removed to make way for country parks were small. A Lord of the Manor would have been unlikely to clear a large village away, as this would have deprived him of tenants' rents, and he would need servants and workers to maintain his house and estates, so in Suffolk, at least, displaced villagers were normally found new accommodation elsewhere.

Culford Heath

Culford Heath, north of Ingham and west of the Bury-Thetford road, is known as 'the forgotten village', the only village in Suffolk that is not signposted and can only be reached by dirt tracks. Some farm workers' cottages were built on the edge of the parish of Culford from the late eighteenth century, and by Victorian times, the settlement had grown into four rows of houses, accommodating thirteen families. Edward Benyon, the owner of Culford Hall, had a school built here and commissioned the architect Arthur Blomfield to design a chapel. Dedicated to St Peter, it was built to the highest specifications, using materials from the Culford Estate, with brilliant stained-glass windows telling the story of St Peter. A curate had responsibility for the area, and regular services, including baptisms, marriages and funerals, were held in the chapel. Inspectors said the school often took more children than it could accommodate.

The school closed in 1945, although Edith Gibson, the schoolmistress, lived there for another twenty years, while the chapel passed from use in 1960. By the 1970s, only three cottages were still inhabited; the school had been taken over by Jan Hretzkun, a Ukrainian ex-patriate. An Italian family lived in one cottage. When I spoke to the father in 1980, he said it was nice not to worry about his children running into the road. (He added that although everybody called Culford Heath 'the forgotten village', the postman still brought the monthly bills.) Dr Leslaw Kwasny, a London doctor of Polish origin, bought the chapel. He and his wife Daguta hoped to turn it into a Polish religious and cultural centre. For its remoteness, Culford Heath was beginning to attract an international population. Legal complications concerning right of way disputes prevented Leslaw from renovating the chapel. Sadly, he died just after they had been resolved.

All the cottages have now been acquired by builders and are being renovated. Even the chapel has been turned into a house; although its Victorian interior will be lost, its exterior, at least, will be preserved. Perhaps life is returning to this little-known corner of the Suffolk Brecklands.

The chapel at Culford Heath.

Derelict cottages at Culford Heath.

Towns Lost to the Sea

For many centuries the Suffolk coast has been menaced by coastal erosion. Easton Barents was once England's easternmost settlement: William Saxton's map of Suffolk, published in 1575, shows it on a promontory extending 1¼ miles into the North Sea, significantly further east than Lowestoft. In Henry VIII's reign, ships of 10 tons could harbour there. There was a parish church, dedicated to St Nicholas, and a separate chapel of St Margaret, which was said to be a centre of local pilgrimage because it contained holy relics. Coastal erosion destroyed Easton Bavents in the seventeenth century, when Hearth Tax returns only recorded seven householders, three of whom were too poor to pay. Some ruins of St Margaret's chapel were still visible in the eighteenth century, but these too have long since vanished into the sea. Now a strip of coastline, Easton Bavents's continued existence as a separate parish is a mere technicality.

When Aldeburgh developed as a fishing port in the sixteenth century, the Moot Hall (now a fascinating museum) stood in the town centre; now it stands on the seafront. Slaughden was the industrial area of Aldeburgh, with a harbour and ship building industry. Even during the Napoleonic Wars it was considered a sufficiently important naval landing point for a Martello Tower to be built there. At the start of the twentieth century, Slaughden still contained twenty-four houses, a pub and a shipbuilder's yard, yet floods were so frequent that a local joke said that the houses had front and back doors so the tide could go in one door and out the other. The last buildings were abandoned in the 1930s, and Slaughden is now a marina for local pleasure boats.

Sizewell was once a twin settlement to Leiston. In 1523, thirty-nine families lived here, versus thirty-three at Leiston. The church, dedicated to St Nicholas, is last mentioned in 1566, when a lame woman was married there, as she could not walk to Leiston. After this, much of Sizewell was lost to coastal erosion. By the eighteenth century, the Sizewell Gap was one

The Martello Tower at Slaughden.

of the wildest and most inaccessible stretches of coast in Suffolk, a favoured rendezvous for smugglers. This led to the establishment of a coastguard station, which became the centre of a sea-fishing hamlet of small houses and wooden shacks.

Sizewell's very remoteness led to its being chosen as the site for nuclear power stations. A Magnox power station (Sizewell A) opened in 1965, and has just ended its useful life. Having produced power for forty-two years, it might require 100 years to be decommissioned. Britain's only pressurised water reactor (Sizewell B) opened in 1987. There are now plans to build two more power stations here (Sizewell C and D). While Britain needs electric power, their presence remains a contentious issue. Is their impact on the landscape necessary? Are they a cost-effective way of producing power? Proponents argue that they provide energy without causing atmospheric pollution. Opponents argue that nuclear power is potentially highly dangerous, that Sizewell B has had an adverse effect on marine life, question the wisdom of building power stations on a coast that is prone to erosion, and continue to campaign for the power stations' closure. The debate is still to be settled.

The Enigma of Covehithe

Covehithe consists of little more than a farmhouse and a ruined church at the end of a narrow road which disappears over the end of a clifftop. Yet it was once a thriving maritime community: the name means 'cove harbour'; it was also called 'North Hales' meaning 'northern neck of land'. The 1327 subsidy (tax) was paid by seventy-two people at Covehithe. As this was only levied on the wealthiest 5% of the population, it suggests that there were as many as 1,400 inhabitants, making it one of Suffolk's ten largest communities. In the fifteenth century, William Yarmouth, a schoolmaster for the sons of local gentry, became vicar

Sizewell, once a fishing village of some importance, now chosen as the location for a pressurised water reactor.

and organised the construction of a great new parish church. In 1523, there were sixty-one taxpaying families, suggesting a community of some size. But the community shrunk, and the villagers were unable to maintain the church. The roof was removed and a small chapel built in the centre of the nave, using fragments of the old church. Plaques on the wall record how the churchwardens 'put it out' (i.e. put a rebuilding contract out to tender).

It could be assumed that the harbour and quayside were destroyed by coastal erosion, while the rest of the village simply disappeared as people moved away. While the church tower was maintained as a seamark, the rest of the church sunk into decay. Only the exterior walls of William Yarmouth's church survive to show the outline of a massive building with a crypt under the chancel and a two-storey porch, contrasting poignantly with the simple thatched chapel within the ruined nave. Beyond this, under the cliffs, a dramatic sweep of empty coastline gives way to salt marshes and heath. Sadly, all Covehithe is now threatened by coastal erosion; in the past decade the sea has encroached considerably, and the area's long-term survival is doubtful. Coastal defences should be considered, for if Covehithe is abandoned to the sea, Suffolk will lose one of its most incredible ruins, not to mention a breathtaking stretch of coastline.

Dunwich

Dunwich, the city which vanished into the sea, is Suffolk's most famous and dramatic lost settlement. The *Domesday Book* showed it as a thriving town with three churches, whose tax assessment included 60,000 herrings, and with a growing population that may have stood at 3,000, making it as large as Bury St Edmunds and Ipswich, and ranking it among England's twenty largest towns. The Dunwich River, running behind the town, and entering the sea to the north, provided an excellent harbour.

The ruins of Covehithe Church, showing the small remains of the village.

The end of the road: the coast road at Covehithe, which disappears over the cliff edge.

Its boundaries were fortified with ditches and palisades. When the Earl of Leicester and Hugh Bigod tried to take Dunwich with a force of Flemish mercenaries in 1173, the townsfolk manned the defences with such determination that they withdrew. At the end of the century, Dunwich received a charter making it a self-governing borough. It was the site of the only Suffolk house of the Knights Templars and one of England's first Franciscan friaries, as well as a Dominican friary; there was also a leper hospital, dedicated to St James, on the edge of the town. By the thirteenth century its population may have grown to 6,000. Containing six parish churches, it returned two Members of Parliament and maintained a mercantile and fishing fleet which traded as far as Iceland and provided warships for the Royal Navy.

The drawback to Dunwich's development was its situation on a shingle cliff. The impressive, high cliffs here gave protection from high tides, but, being wholly composed of sand and stones, they could easily be washed away. The *Domesday Book* ominously recorded that half the town's agricultural land had been lost to the sea in the previous ten years. During the thirteenth century, when Dunwich stood at the height of its prosperity, the haven had to repeatedly be re-cut as storms and high tides continuously obstructed it with mud and shingle. Climatologists believe that a 'mini ice age' began in the fourteenth century, marked by lowering temperatures, wetter weather and rising sea levels. This could not have done Dunwich any favours. By 1350 continuing storms had permanently blocked the harbour, moved the river mouth to Walberswick, and destroyed a whole sector of the town, including three parish churches. This could have marked a change in the townspeople's collective psychology. While Dunwich was still one of Suffolk's larger towns, the overriding concern was not to develop or expand it, but to try and hold on to its shrinking fortunes. At the start of the Tudor period, its population was still over 1,000, but a fresh series of storms and renewed coastal erosion caused a fourth church to vanish. Dunwich's last hurrah as a naval base occurred when it sent one pinnace to the fleet that met the Spanish Armada.

The cliffs at Dunwich.

The ruins of Greyfriars convent and All Saints' Church at Dunwich. (The church has been lost to the sea.)

When Charles I introduced a new tax called 'Ship Money', Dunwich was only charged £4, the smallest sum asked from any seaport, and it was so poor that this was cut to £2. When the sea reached the Market Place, the Market Cross, Town Hall and a fifth church were demolished, since there was no way of saving them.

In the eighteenth century, All Saints', Dunwich's last church, was abandoned. Its population fell to 100, which included between fifteen and forty 'freemen' who operated a vestigial Borough Corporation and elected two Members of Parliament. Dunwich became a 'Rotten Borough' where MPs obtained office for their own benefit, through open bribery and corruption. The Downing family acquired land there so they could serve as MPs, before being replaced by an alliance of the Barne family of Sotterley and the Vanneck family of Heveningham. This was not wholly to the freemen's disadvantage, as they received reduced rents and regular banquets in return for their votes, until the Reform Act of 1832 effectively abolished 'Rotten Boroughs'. An anachronistic Borough Corporation, operating from a small Town Hall (still standing near the Ship pub) was wound up in 1882; the borough's last 'freeman' died in 1936.

Yet, as Dunwich shed its last trappings of civic grandeur, it revived as a village. The Barne family financed the building of a new church, along with model cottages for their tenants. The first Franciscan friary was lost to the sea; its replacement was prudently built further inland, and the ruins can be explored. The ruins of St James's Leper Hospital stand in the modern churchyard. After the tower of the medieval church of All Saints' fell over the cliff, the last corner buttress was removed to the new churchyard, as were some gravestones; other gravestones still stand on the clifftop and rubble from the church can be seen on the beach at low tide. A museum of the town's history opened in 1935; its collections have been enlarged by marine archaeologists. A seaside fish and chip shop is legendary among connoisseurs of this meal. Woods, heaths and marshes surrounding the village form nature reserves. For an alternative seaside outing, no location in England can provide more enjoyment than Dunwich.

9

INDUSTRY AND ENTERPRISE

Although Suffolk is often regarded as an agricultural county, it developed an industrial base in the Middle Ages; much of this was inevitably based on agriculture, but some quite surprising initiatives have taken place.

Wool-Cloth and Textiles

From the fourteenth century, south Suffolk developed as a centre of wool-cloth production. Manufacture took place in a region stretching in an arc from East Bergholt, through Glemsford, to Clare, with outlying centres in Bury St Edmunds and Haverhill. It could be argued that this was the first region of England to industrialise. It has never been satisfactorily explained why this happened, but over several generations, the region acquired the most important necessity for any industry: a pool of skilled and experienced labour.

Clothiers oversaw the production of wool-cloth. Much wool came from East Anglian flocks of Norfolk Horn sheep. This was carded into fibre and then spun into yarn by women and children. Spun wool was normally dyed blue, using woad, before being woven into cloth (giving rise to the expression 'dyed in the wool'). Cloth was then sent for fulling, to be soaked and beaten in water mixed with fuller's earth to clean and strengthen it. Next it was dried and stretched on frames called tenters (hence the expression 'to wait on tenterhooks'). An area east of Lavenham Church is called Tenter Piece, while Hadleigh cricket ground stands on Tainter Meadow, named after this process. London was the greatest mart for sale of wool-cloth, from where much was exported to the Netherlands, France, Germany, the Baltic and even North Africa.

The standard Suffolk wool-cloth was a broadcloth which was 84½ft long and 63in wide, requiring two people to weave it. In 1468 Hadleigh, Lavenham and Bury produced 56 miles of broadcloth. Kersey produced a narrow cloth, 72ft long and 37in wide, which could be made by a single weaver (giving rise to the name 'Kersey' for narrow wool-cloth). Glemsford was known for undyed white cloth, called Glaynesford. Suffolk wool-cloth was regarded as being coarse and of poor quality but it sold well because of its relative cheapness.

Among the Suffolk wool-cloth towns, Lavenham had the most spectacular rise and fall. It was a manor of the de Vere family, who were Earls of Oxford, with their principal residence just over

The Guildhall of Corpus Christi in Lavenham Market Place, the centre of the town's cloth industry, now opened to the public by the National Trust.

the county boundary at Castle Hedingham in Essex. Hugh de Vere, the fifth Earl of Oxford, obtained the right to start a market there in 1257, and it has been suggested that the de Veres used their influence to promote and develop Lavenham, which reached the height of its fortunes after John de Vere, the thirteenth Earl of Oxford, led Henry VII's army to victory at the Battle of Bosworth. John de Vere and the Lavenham clothiers collaborated to fund the construction of a magnificent parish church as a confident statement of their prosperity and importance. By the start of Henry VIII's reign, Lavenham was among England's twenty wealthiest towns. Industrial and human activity created waste and pollution, so the Lavenham clothiers set up an underground sewer system, which still survives; although access is difficult, it is one of Europe's earliest waste-disposal systems. Thomas Spring, its greatest clothier, became the wealthiest non-noble person in England, buying land in a hundred Suffolk manors and marrying one of his daughters to the de Vere family. The seventeenth Earl dissipated the family fortunes and sold his Lavenham property, while the Springs (and many other clothiers) retired from business to live as country gentlemen. By the end of the Tudor age Lavenham was a town in decline.

During the Elizabethan era, Continental wars disrupted export markets, while the new draperies, colourful, lightweight wool-cloth, introduced by immigrants from the Netherlands, replaced Suffolk wool-cloth in popularity. Lavenham, and many other Suffolk towns, ended up processing raw wool for the new textile centres.

South Suffolk was the first part of England to de-industrialise. Ironically, this ensured the preservation of the region's incredible heritage of medieval and Tudor architecture. There was enough activity to ensure that existing buildings could be maintained, but not enough wealth to permit their replacement, leading to the region's revival as a centre of the tourist and heritage industries in the twentieth century.

Haverhill became a centre for the production of drabbet, a linen/cotton mix, used to make agricultural workers' smocks. Daniel Gurteen became a clothier in Haverhill in 1784. His grandson Daniel (known as Daniel Gurteen Junior) opened the Chauntry Mill factory in

1819. Diversifying into other forms of clothing and textiles, by the end of the century the Gurteens employed 3,000 people. Haverhill's Victorian development was due to the Gurteens, who financed the building of the ostentatious Town Hall (now an excellent arts and local history centre) and (as they were Congregationalists) the Congregational church, the town's largest public building. The Gurteen family still operate their clothing company from the Chauntry Mill factory.

In the Victorian era the weaving of horsehair and coir (coconut husk fibre) were introduced to Long Melford, Lavenham and Glemsford. Horeshair was used for stuffing furniture, particularly railway carriage seats. William Witingham Roper became the country's largest producer, advertising his Lavenham factory as the sole supplier to the Houses of Parliament. Weaving was done by women; a roll of horsehair cloth (a piece) was 52ft long, containing 120 hairs an inch. Work was incredibly painstaking, leading to a Lavenham expression: 'Mother will pay when she fells' (i.e. completes her roll of cloth).

Coir could be turned into hard-wearing mats. Weaving, which required some physical strength, was carried out by men. The Suffolk coir industry's finest hour came in 1906, when the Glemsford factories produced the world's largest ever carpet: 3,000 sq. ft, for London's Olympia Centre.

The Suffolk horsehair and coir-weaving industries collapsed in the 1930s with the Depression, the invention of chemical-based furniture stuffing and floor covering, and cheaper imports from Asia and Africa. Arnold & Gould, Britain's last horsehair factory, in Glemsford, made brushes, violin bows and barristers' wigs, but closed in 1982. This and other former factory buildings in the High Street and the Brent Eleigh Road at Lavenham have been converted into flats. Coconut House, the former centre of the Long Melford coir-weaving industry, stands south of the village school, opposite the Bull Hotel in the High Street.

The British silk industry was confined to London until magistrates were empowered to set weavers' wages in 1774. Several silk manufacturers moved to Suffolk, where wages were not regulated, although the reduced wages they offered were still higher than those paid by wool manufacturers. Production spread to Mildenhall, but was eventually concentrated in Sudbury. Three-storey weavers' houses, with large, well-lit middle floors to accommodate silk looms, were built along Melford Road and in Weaver's Lane. The Gainsborough Silk Weaving Company (which produces silk for royal functions), Stephen Walters and Vanner's have turned Sudbury into Britain's largest producer of silk.

Windmills and Watermills

Suffolk contains an exceptional heritage of wind and watermills. Flatford watermill was the home of the artist John Constable, whose pictures of the building have made it world famous. Other Suffolk mills are important examples of industrial archaeology.

The earliest English windmills were post mills, where the body (or buck) was supported on an oak post and turned to face the wind. Brick tower mills were a later development, where sails were installed into a cap, which revolved to face the wind.

Dendrochronology has dated the buck of a post mill at Drinkstone to 1587 and other timbers to the sixteenth century, suggesting that it is the oldest post mill in the country. (Drinkstone post mill features in 'Don't Forget The Diver', a 1970 episode of the television sitcom *Dad's Army*, when the platoon has to take it in a military exercise.) Mills at Friston and Framsden are respectively 51 and 48ft high, Britain's tallest post mills. Many mill enthusiasts regard Saxtead post mill (now opened by English Heritage) as the perfect example of its kind.

Saxtead post mill.

A tower mill at Bardwell was restored to operational order until the sails were wrecked in a hurricane. The owners and a dedicated group of supporters are now working to restore the mill so it can continue to grind flour again.

Pakenham is the only parish in England to contain a working windmill and watermill. A tower mill was built in about 1831 by the Heffer family. Michael Bryant still grinds animal feed here; at eighty, he has recently published *A Touch Of The Wind*, memoirs of life as a mill owner. The eighteenth-century watermill stands where the Blackbourne River enters Pakenham Fen. Archaeological excavations have uncovered Tudor foundations below the floor, and the *Domesday Book* recorded a mill at Pakenham, suggesting that there was a watermill here in Anglo-Saxon times. The Suffolk Preservation Society now opens Pakenham watermill to the public.

Woodbridge possesses Britain's only remaining operational tide mill. As the tide came up the River Deben, a pool beside the mill was allowed to fill; when the tide went out, the wheel was engaged and turned by the water's outward flow. It was saved from demolition by Jean

Framsden windwill.

Gardner, a Suffolk woman, who bought it and restored it with the help of volunteers. A small area of the mill pond has been kept to power the mill. If you time your visit to coincide with the ebb tide, you will have the (great) enjoyment of seeing the mill in action.

Brandon Gunflints

The Brandon flint-knapping industry developed during the eighteenth century, after high-quality flint strata were found near the town. These proved ideal for flintlock rifles. Flint miners usually worked individually, digging narrow 40ft shafts, which they filled when exhausted. Flints were knapped (struck) into shape in workshops in Brandon, where a skilled flintknapper could produce 300 gunflints an hour. During the Napoleonic Wars, 200 Brandon flintknappers supplied the Duke of Wellington's armies with up to 1½ million gunflints a month. The development of the percussion gun caused a rapid decline in the Brandon flint industry, although flints continued to be exported to Africa and Asia, where older rifles were still in use. Even in the twentieth century there was a small market, supplying vintage firearm enthusiasts, but Arthur 'Pony' Ashley, the last Ling Heath miner, died in 1936, and Fred Avery, the last Brandon gunflint manufacturer, died in 1996. Exhibits on the industry can be seen in the Brandon Heritage Centre.

Lowestoft Porcelain

A consortium of local businessmen and landowners cooperated to open a porcelain factory in Bell Lane (modern Crown Street) at Lowestoft in 1760. It specialised in small items of 'soft paste' china (fired at 1100c rather than 1350-1450c as is normal with commoner 'hard

Woodbridge tide mill.

Specimens of Lowestoft porcelain. (Reproduced by permission of the Lowestoft Museum)

paste china'). These were hand painted with blue designs, some including the words 'A trifle from Lowestoft' and showing local views – the world's first local souvenirs. The factory was among the first to improve its business by offering tours to interested visitors. Some products were sent to London and even the Netherlands. The factory was managed by a father and son, both called Robert Browne. (A story says that one of them worked in a factory at Bow in London, and hid under a barrel to watch the factory owners preparing the next day's work, so as to learn their secret techniques.) The Lowestoft factory employed 100 workers; women received the same wages as male employees if their skills warranted it. The factory closed in 1799; possibly it was unable to compete with the Staffordshire factories. Some of the workforce migrated to the Worcester potteries, where they became highly regarded craftsmen. Now highly collectable, good selections of Lowestoft porcelain can be seen in the Lowestoft Museum and Christchurch Mansion in Ipswich.

Garretts of Leiston

Richard Garrett took over a blacksmith's forge at Leiston in 1778, which eventually employed eight men. His son, Richard Garrett II, began making threshing machines, and his son, Richard Garrett III, became an internationally famous manufacturer of agricultural machinery, including traction engines. As a prominent participant in the Great Exhibition of 1851, he saw American technology in operation, and decided to use US 'production line' methods. He had a workshop called the 'Long Shop' built at Leiston, where portable steam engines could be built piece by piece: the world's first assembly line factory. Leiston's growth from a village into a town was due to Richard Garrett III.

The Long Shop at Leiston, looking down from the gallery. (Reproduced by permission of the Long Shop Museum)

During the twentieth century Garrett's began manufacturing electric vehicles (including dustcarts for the city of Glasgow). Its decline is said to have begun after the Russian Revolution, when the Bolsheviks repudiated the Tsarist government's debts of over £200,000. It amalgamated with several similar companies to form 'Agricultural and General Engineers'. This collapsed during the Depression, after which Garrett's was bought out by larger organisations, until its eventual closure in 1980. Surviving factory buildings, including the Long Shop, are now part of a brilliant museum displaying the company's history and products.

Ransomes of Ipswich

Robert Ransome, a Quaker, opened a forge in Old Foundry Road in Ipswich in 1789. At the start of the nineteenth century, he revolutionised agriculture and metallurgy by discovering the 'chilling' process, where newly forged ploughs were moved from a furnace and cooled quickly, thus creating a hard under and soft upper surface which remained sharp with normal use. Robert began making ploughs to standard designs with matching components, so that if one part was broken or damaged, the farmer could buy a replacement part, rather than a new plough, originating the spare parts industry.

The Ransome family continued to run the firm. When Edward Budding and John Ferrabee of Stroud in Gloucestershire patented the first practical design for a lawnmower, they purchased the rights to manufacture these, to become the world's first and largest lawnmower manufacturer. Entering the railway industry, they patented trenails and chairs, which held railway lines in place, manufacturing over 30 million. In 1842 they produced the first traction engine, a self-propelling steam engine that could travel over roads and open countryside, revolutionising transport.

The firm was divided into two companies. Ransomes and Rapier handled railway operations; its early contracts included the first railway in China. It eventually fell into the clutches of the nefarious Robert Maxwell, who closed it and demolished its waterside works. Ransomes, Sims and Jeffries produced agricultural machinery and lawnmowers from the Orwell Works by Ipswich docks; during the First World War 5,000 men and women worked there. This company later moved to Nacton, but sold its agricultural division, before being taken over by Textron, an American company, under which name they still produce lawnmowers.

Ransomes' traction engine and threshing machine on display at the Museum of East Anglian Life at Stowmarket.

There is a permanent exhibition on the history of the Ransomes companies in the Museum of East Anglian Life at Stowmarket, while some vehicles they made can be seen at the Ipswich Transport Museum.

Fertilizer Production

The discovery of coprolite deposits below East Suffolk led to the development of a fertilizer industry. Coprolites are a Greensand mineral deposit with a high phosphate content. The name was devised by the geologist William Buckland, who believed it to be fossilised dinosaur droppings. There is a tradition that a Levington farmer called Edmund Edwards found deposits under his farm in 1718, and ground them to fertilise his fields. When holidaying at Felixstowe (then a small fishing village) in 1843, John Stevens Henslow, a Cambridge professor who had become rector of Hitcham, discovered coprolite deposits in the cliffs, leading to extraction there, and at Trimley, Alderton, Bawdsey, Kirton and Newbourn.

Edward Packard, a chemist, began grinding coprolites in a mill at Snape, then dissolving them in acid. He moved his operations to the Ipswich quayside, but they generated a smell that was considered too offensive, even for a dockyard, and he relocated to Bramford, by the Gipping (then canalised). His brief operation at Ipswich is commemorated by Coprolite Street, which ran beside his factory.

Joseph Fison, a miller, began grinding coprolites in Ipswich, and also moved to Bramford: the Packard and Fison factories were only separated by a brick wall. Two brothers, Edward and Eustace Prentice, set up another phosphate works at Stowmarket.

From the 1870s Suffolk factories began importing phosphates from the Continent. After the First World War, Packard's, Fison's and Prentice's merged, allegedly taking the name Fison's because while Packard and Prentice sales representatives travelled by bicycle, Fison representatives were better known as they used automobiles and covered a wider area. Fison's diversified into the manufacture of other fertilisers and continued as a leading manufacturer, until a takeover by Norsk Hydro. The Bramford factory was saved by a management buyout, and renamed Levington Horticulture (since Fison's had a branch there, although was there any realisation that the Suffolk fertiliser industry started at Levington?) but the Bramford works and the Suffolk fertiliser industry finally closed in 2003.

Printing in Bungay and Beccles

Richard Morris opened a printing works in Bungay in 1794 and was joined by Charles Brightly. The business prospered enormously after they invited John Childs, a Norwich grocer's assistant, to join them. He initiated the 'Imperial Edition of Standard Authors', the first production of classic literature in cheap format, and began publishing cheap reference works. A Congregationalist, John Childs objected to the fact that in England only the king's printer was allowed to print the Bible. He side-stepped the law by publishing low-cost Biblical texts with footnotes and annotations. Still feeling strongly on the issue, he helped to set up an enquiry that led to the ending of the king's printer's monopoly of Bible production.

Richard Clay, a London printer, later took over the Bungay works, renaming it the Chaucer Press. The Richard Clay Company eventually moved its entire operation to Bungay (from where it printed some of the first Penguin Books). The St Ives group rescued it from a hostile takeover bid by Robert Maxwell, and it is now Britain's largest single printing works, producing the *Harry Potter* books.

The Caxton Press was established at Beccles in the nineteenth century. William Clowes was a leading London printer, and in 1873, two of his sons went into partnership with William Moore, the proprietor of the Caxton Works. Soon afterwards William Moore absconded with £40,000 of company funds (he was later apprehended and sentenced to five years hard labour). Despite this, Clowes and Clowes at Beccles became one of the largest provincial printers, before amalgamating with their father's firm. After the Second World War, the company relocated to Beccles, where it now prints ten million books a year, including such standard works as *Whitaker's Almanac* and *Who's Who*. Exhibits on Clowes and the Caxton Works can be seen in the Beccles Museum.

Dockyards

Ipswich's prosperity has often fluctuated as the Orwell's upper reaches are prone to silting and difficult to navigate. In 1836 it was decided to overcome these difficulties by digging a 33-acre wet dock, then the largest in the world. Throughout the nineteenth century, this served over 1,000 ships a year. Ransome's engineering companies and the Suffolk fertiliser industry owed much of their growth to the docks. As ships grew in the 1970s, the Port of Ipswich moved downriver, and the dock is now being developed as an urban amenity and heritage attraction.

Lowestoft lacked a harbour until 1827, when a group of entrepreneurs devised a navigation scheme to link it with Norwich. This proved inefficient and the harbour, which rapidly silted up, was regarded as a white elephant until 1843, when Samuel Morton Peto bought it.

The Ipswich Custom House, built in 1845 as a statement of the town's renewed importance as a port.

Fishing ships leaving Lowestoft harbour.

Felixstowe docks as seen from Freston.

A building contractor, at thirty-three Samuel Morton Peto had constructed Trafalgar Square and the Houses of Parliament. He had the harbour rebuilt, extending the dock walls to prevent silting, and linked Lowestoft with the new railway network, making a promise that fish which were landed in Lowestoft would be in Manchester the same day. Soon over 30 million herring were landed at Lowestoft each year. Packing ice was pulled in great floes from Norway and stored in quayside warehouses. Samuel opened a steamer link with Denmark, although he was unable to find sufficient support for a scheme to build a canal across Jutland and make Lowestoft the hub of Anglo-Baltic trade. Although a truly honest and honourable man, Samuel went bankrupt, but he left modern Lowestoft as his memorial. Lowestoft's great year as a fishing port was 1913, when over 700 ships bought over 500 million herring into port. The development of trawler fishing and depletion of North Sea fish stocks, followed by EU regulations, caused the herring fisheries' decline from the 1960s, but other forms of commercial fishing are carried out here, and the port also services the North Sea oil industry.

George Tomline, a wealthy Victorian (who assumed the honorary title of 'Colonel' after a brief military career) bought land along the lower shores of the Orwell. In 1877 he financed a private rail link to Felixstowe, envisioning its development as a holiday resort and dockyard. Unfortunately, he died in 1889, three years after Felixstowe dock was completed. The Great Eastern Railway bought out the railway line, after which Felixstowe developed into a fashionable holiday resort, but the docks were neglected in favour of the railway company's existing dock and ferry terminal at Harwich. Felixstowe docks remained a forgotten backwater until 1951, when Gordon Parker acquired it and began expanding its facilities. Felixstowe was the first British port to adopt the new idea of transporting cargos by container. Now handling over a third of the UK's container traffic, it is one of Europe's busiest and most active commercial ports.

10

ALL CREATURES GREAT AND SMALL

Newmarket

No Suffolk town is more identified with animals than Newmarket, which owes its origin as a horse-racing centre to James I, finding Newmarket Heath excellent for hawking and hare coursing, visited it regularly. The first recorded horse-race at Newmarket took place in 1622, between horses owned by the Earl of Salisbury and the Duke of Buckingham, for £100, which the Earl's horse won. Charles I had a stand built on the Heath from which he could watch these races. Charles II visited Newmarket twice a year, starting the traditional summer and autumn meetings. He opened the Palace House stables to breed and train horses, now the world's oldest racing stable; in 1665 he founded the Newmarket Town Plate, the oldest continually run horse-race in the world. The Jockey Club, founded by wealthy patrons of horse-racing, moved to Newmarket in 1752, to become British horse-racing's governing body.

Horse-races at Newmarket now attract an international audience. Summer meetings are held on the July course, autumn meetings on the Rowley Mile. (Charles II called his favourite stallion Old Rowley; this name was transferred to Charles, for his many female liaisons, and then to the racecourse.) Up to 5000 horses are stabled in Newmarket and the surrounding area (the number varies over the year). Sixty-five stud farms, including the National Stud, Tattersall's, Europe's largest horse auctioneer and many organisations dedicated to the breeding and care of horses are based here. The Jockey Club maintains 2,500 acres of heathland for training (coincidentally preserving Newmarket Heath) with over 80 miles of gallops and traffic-free walking tracks around the town. From the town's population of 15,000, the horse industry directly employs 2,000. Some aspects of the town's racing heritage can be discovered in the National Museum of Horse-racing in Newmarket.

The First Steeplechase

There is a popular story that Suffolk was the setting for the world's first steeplechase. The

Racehorses being exercised by the Devil's Ditch, an Anglo-Saxon earthwork on Newmarket Heath.

tale goes that one night in 1803, a group of army officers, stationed at Ipswich during the Napoleonic Wars, raced their horses across country, over hedges, fences, ditches and streams, as much for an adventure as a contest, with the steeple of Nacton Church as their destination. The expression steeplechase has become synonymous with a horse-race across open countryside or a rough track, but while the story is part of horseriding folklore, there is some doubt about the details of the story, and steeplechasing may have originated spontaneously in several locations.

Suffolk Punches

The country's native workhorse, the Suffolk Horse, better known as 'Suffolk Punches', were Britain's strongest working horses. Distinguished by their red or sorrel colour, described as chesnut (the missing 't' is intentional) they also display a white 'star', 'blaze' or 'shim' down the muzzle. Unusually tall and bulky, the name 'Punch' derives from an archaic usage meaning a stout, fat man (*vide* Punch and Judy). Another feature are their 'clean' lower legs, with short hair, which do not become caked with earth when working the land.

By Elizabethan times they were being bred in the county's south-east Sandling area, where the light soil could be cultivated more effectively by horse-drawn ploughs than the ox plough commonly used at the time. All Suffolk Punches now trace their ancestry to a horse bred by Thomas Crisp of Chillesford's 'Horse of Ufford 404', foaled in 1768. The Suffolk Horse Society was formed a century later to ensure the breed's purity and promote its use. Known for strength, but also gentleness and patience, a Suffolk Punch fed before dawn could often work nine hours with only short breaks. Since Suffolk horses were bred for endurance rather than speed, farmers held drawing contests, where the horse that pulled a heavy load a set distance with the fewest 'tifters' (stops) was the winner.

During the First World War, Suffolk Punches were used for transport in the trenches.

Suffolk Punches, George and Boxer, aged nine and twelve, at a Suffolk Horse Society event at Easton Park in 2006.

Suffolk Punches at a ploughing contest organised by the Suffolk Horse Society at Bucklesham in 2007.

Ray Hubbard, a veteran Suffolk horseman, told me that one was seen to pull a munitions wagon that normally required four horses to move it. After the war, they were replaced by agricultural machines, and less than 200 were left by the 1970s. The breed might have died out without the dedication of the Suffolk Horse Society and a few enthusiasts. The propagation of the breed was in a large measure carried out at Colony Farm at Hollesley, which had been acquired by the Prison Service to rehabilitate prisoners, in particular young offenders, by teaching them agricultural skills. Suffolk Punches had been bred at Colony Farm for over a century, and work with horses was found to be highly beneficial to inmates. When the prison service decided to sell Colony Farm, the Suffolk Punch Trust was formed to buy it and continue its work.

At the time of writing the UK population of Suffolk Punches is roughly 420 (although 100 are geldings) with twenty-six licensed stallions and roughly 170 breeding mares: there are more Giant Pandas in the world today, but it can be hoped that the breed has attracted enough supportive interest to ensure its continuation. The Suffolk Horse Society runs an admirable museum in its headquarters in Woodbridge's Elizabethan Town Hall and organises regular events across the county, where these horses can be seen.

Suffolk Dun Poll Cattle

The north-western part of East Suffolk was known for the Suffolk Dun Poll cow, so called as it was a dun (brownish-grey) colour and polled (lacked horns). Although comparatively small and rather ungainly in appearance, individual cows might give eight gallons of milk a day, making them, for their size, England's best milk producers. In the nineteenth century, Suffolk Dun Polls were cross-bred with Norfolk red cows to produce Red Poll cattle, which replaced both breeds across East Anglia. In 1904, the last herd of twenty-five was brought by Arthur Wakerley of Gedding Hall. Sold off and dispersed over the next decade, they passed into extinction.

The last herd of Suffolk Dun Poll cattle at Gedding Hall.

Suffolk Sheep

Unlike the Suffolk Punch and Dun Poll, the Suffolk black-faced sheep has proliferated enormously. From the Middle Ages, Suffolk farmers generally reared Norfolk horn sheep (so called from their prominent curly horns), first bred in the Brecklands. The Suffolk black-faced sheep's origin can be traced quite precisely to 1784, when the agriculturalist Arthur Young acquired a Southdown ram for his Bradfield Combust farm. Southdowns, originating in Sussex, lack horns, and are more docile than Norfolks, but this particular Southdown was not wholly submissive, as he got loose among a neighbour's flock of Norfolk ewes. The many resulting lambs were thought to be fatter and gentler than Norfolks, and selective breeding began. Suffolk black-faces have become one of Britain's most popular sheep; there are now over 1000,000 in the British Isles.

In passing, it should be added that by 1968, only six Norfolk Horns had survived. Fears for their continued existence helped lead to the formation of the Rare Breeds Survival Trust, dedicated to preserving historic farm animals. The Norfolk Horn was re-established by cross-breeding with Suffolk and Welsh Lleyn sheep, and several dedicated enthusiasts now maintain flocks, the largest being at Kentwell Hall.

Endangered Insects and Spiders

For most of the twentieth century, the Pashford pot beetle, named from its practice of making small clay pots to live in, was only known at Pashford Poors Fen at Lakenheath (a Suffolk Wildlife Trust nature reserve), but it has not been seen since 2002, and is now listed as a 'missing species'. Pashford Poors Fen is also the only site in Britain where the leaf beetle can be found, an insect about which little is known apart from the fact that it eats sorrel.

A shepherd boy with Suffolk black-face sheep at Timworth in 1906.

Levi, a Norfolk Horn Ram. Born as part of the Kentwell flock, he was so named as his registration number was 501. Levi later moved to Sascombe Vineyards, across the county border, to Kirtling in Cambridgeshire. Although occasionally grumpy and temperamental, he could also be very loyal, affectionate and friendly. He lived to be 26, the oldest ram in England.

The fen raft spider was unknown in Britain until 1956, when a colony was discovered at Redgrave and Lopham Fen. It seems surprising that it had never been observed before, as it is one of the largest European spiders; females have brown and white striped bodies ¾in long and a 2in leg span. Smaller colonies have since been discovered near Swansea in Wales and Pevensey in Sussex, but its appearance at Redgrave Fen is puzzling, as the ponds it inhabits are not natural, but were created by peat digging.

Redgrave Fen was in danger of drying out due to water extraction, and the fen raft spider colony was reduced to two ponds when the Suffolk Wildlife Trust and English Nature initiated a species recovery programme. Water levels were restored, and research is taking place in ways to revive the colony. Arachnophobics need not be deterred from visiting Redgrave Fen, which is a most attractive, enjoyable and environmentally significant nature reserve, since the fen raft spider hibernates between October and March, and even when active, still confines itself to one clearly signposted area of the fen.

Animals as Nature Conservation Agents

When seeking a way to clear the most overgrown and waterlogged areas of Redgrave and Lopham Fen, the Suffolk Wildlife Trust imported Polish Konik ponies. Descended from the Tarpan, the wild horse of central Asia and Eastern Europe, Koniks preserve a robust temperament, which allows them to live in wet conditions and winter outdoors. Five were imported from Oostvaardersplassen Nature Reserve in the Netherlands, and five more from Poland. They immediately adapted to their new home. Able to go up to their bellies to graze,

Konik ponies at Redgrave and Lopham Fen.

they soon cleared areas that the hardiest human volunteers and the strongest machinery could not reach. Since they included one stallion, they soon increased to twenty-eight, some of which were sold to the Royal Society for the Protection of Birds (RSPB) reserves at Minsmere and the Hen Reedbeds near Southwold.

The RSPB recently borrowed five Exmoor ponies from the Rare Breeds Survival Trust to clear vegetation from Snape Warren and its Suffolk coastal reserves. They have proved so successful that the Society is now looking for an Exmoor stallion so they can breed more.

The RSPB also uses Manx Loaghtan sheep to clear vegetation on some Suffolk nature reserves. Meanwhile, the Suffolk Wildlife Trust employs a flying flock of Hebridean sheep at Melton, which is moved around reserves in the coastal and sandling areas as required.

The White Bull of Bury

In medieval Bury St Edmunds, if a married woman wished to become a mother, she walked beside a white bull, who was garlanded with flowers, following the monks of Bury in procession, after which she prayed for a child at St Edmund's shrine. A bull was kept for this procession on the Haberden, a meadow near Southgate Street, where he lived a comfortable life, free from toil. The practice ceased at the Dissolution. As a bull is a symbol of strength, virility and sexual prowess, it could be understood why one was used in this way. Although it cannot be proved, it is tempting to think that the custom harked back to a pre-Christian practice.

Bull Baiting

Bull baiting remained inexplicably popular in Suffolk, often taking place on 5 November, (Guy Fawkes Day). On 7 November 1793 the *Bury Post* reported how a bull tethered for baiting with dogs in Bury broke loose, gored and injured several spectators, and was not caught until it reached Pakenham. It would be interesting to know if people who enjoyed watching animals attacking each other gained enjoyment when the animals attacked them. The following week the *Bury Post* reported that the Borough Council would prosecute anybody who tried to continue bull baiting in the town, thus ending the practice there.

On 10 November 1841 a correspondent complained to the *Bury Post* that bull baiting continued at Lavenham. The law at the time could not prevent animal cruelty, but only punish those who had inflicted suffering upon an animal, so the following November Henry Thomas, the secretary of the Royal Society for the Prevention of Cruelty to Animals arrived with two police constables. They identified thirteen organisers and leading participants, who were summoned to court and offered the alternative of fines of up to £5 or up to two months' imprisonment with hard labour. Five paid fines, which were given to Lavenham National School, and eight were imprisoned. This represented the last case of bull-baiting in England, a custom whose passing can cause no regret.

Briton, the Lion of Boxford

George Smith, better known as 'Tornado Smith', the son of the proprietor of the White Hart Inn at Boxford, was the leading rider of the 'Wall of Death', a motorcycle stunt show. In 1933 Tornado bought a female lion cub from Chapman's Circus. Calling her Briton, he trained her to ride in his sidecar while he performed on his motorcycle. When not touring or performing, Tornado kept Briton in a cage at the White Hart and took her for walks around Boxford on a lead. There are several conflicting stories about her death in 1938: that she broke a leg, or became old or aggressive and had to be put down, or that somebody saw Briton playing with Tornado, thought she was attacking him, and shot her. She was buried under the front lawn of the White Hart, under a memorial (now vanished) which read:

> BRITON
> The wall of death she rode with safety,
> In her cage she met her doom.

Animal Memorials

Acton Place was built in the eighteenth century for Robert Jennens, although the last remnants were demolished after the Second World War. The *Suffolk Free Press* of 10 September 1952 reported that builders clearing the site found some broken masonry, including a stone with the inscription:

> Here lyeth Dutchess the Dam of the Setting dogs, favourite and constant companion of her master and dyde 13 days after him on the 10th March 1725

In a brick vault nearby were the skeletons of two dogs. Robert's son, William, became notoriously miserly in his later years, but was still devoted to his dogs. Local tradition held that

The village sign at Boxford, showing Tornado Smith on a motorcycle with Briton in his sidecar.

he took his favourite dog, a setter, on visits to London. On what would be his last trip, he left it at home. The day after his departure, it had vanished from Acton Place. Three days later it appeared, dying, at his London house. It is thought that William had his favourite dog buried with his father's pet.

A plaque on a wall in the grounds of Euston Hall reads: 'Trouncer 1788 Foxes rejoice, here buried lies your foe.' Trouncer was a favourite dog of the third Duke of Grafton, who was prime minister to George III. Robert Bloomfield mentions him in *The Farmer's Boy* with the lines:

Pride of thy race! With worth far less than thine
Full many human leaders daily shine!
No flowers are strewn around ambition's car:
An honest dogs a nobler theme by far.

An adjoining plaque reads: 'Garland 1799 The spotless rival of his grandsire's fame.' A third plaque honours 'A faithful and singularly intelligent spaniel' who was accidentally shot in the park in 1813 'while performing her duty'.

Hardwick Hall, the home of the Cullum family, near Bury St Edmunds, was demolished in 1925, but the surrounding park was kept as a public open space. When the West Suffolk Hospital was built on the southern perimeter of the park, the development missed a small dog's cemetery in a corner of a car park, roughly ¼ mile north-east of St Nicholas Hospice. Rather overgrown, and hard to find, it contains five stones, including 'Poor old Dandie', 'Poor Blind Peter', 'Ching' and his faithful wife, 'Fanny'.

Thornham Walks contains the Henniker family's pet cemetery. Two stones list dogs, others name horses, including Bob and Mahuta, who served at the Battle of Tel-el-Kebir, and Toto, who served in several engagements during the Boer War. Since the park's restoration, the Hennikers have added a new stone to a black Alsatian with the ominous name Dracula. A nearby memorial to the sixth Baron Henniker includes bas-relief carvings of his three favourite dogs.

Helmingham Hall's beautiful gardens include a cemetery for the Tollemache family's dogs, with sixteen headstones from 1960 onwards.

The statue of a dog called Snooks stands on the sea front at Aldeburgh, near the Moot Hall Museum. Snook's pet humans, Patrick (better known as Robin) Acheson and his wife, Nora were local doctors. As a town councillor, Robin was responsible for turning a nearby military water tank into a model boating pond. Nora, the first woman to accompany a lifeboat crew, maintained Aldeburgh's medical services during the Second World War. The statue was commissioned as a memorial to Robin and unveiled by his granddaughters; an inscription to Nora was added later. On the front wall of 171 Main Street there is a dog's drinking fountain, opened in 1948, which bears the rhyme:

Drink, Doggie drink, man is your debtor
And you never present your bill,
But faithful serve, for worse, for better,
Drink, Doggie, drink your fill.

Black Shuck

Black Shuck is the legendary phantom dog of Suffolk. A giant creature with burning eyes, he entered Suffolk folklore in 1577, during a storm of legendary ferocity, when the towers of St Mary's Church at Bungay and Blythburgh Church were badly damaged by lightning. A pamphlet entitled *A Strange and Terrible Wonder* was published, stating that the Devil had appeared and wreaked havoc in both churches in the form of a black dog. A nineteenth-century reprint included a poem with such immortal lines as:

The pet cemetery at Thornham Walks.

Memorial to Snooks at Aldeburgh.

All down the church in midst of fire
The hellish monster flew
And passing onward to the quire
He many people slew.

Scorch marks on the north nave door at Blythburgh are said to have been made as the dog fled the church. The legend has left an impression on Bungay, where he appears on the town's coat of arms, while local athletics teams call themselves Black Dogs.

Reports say that Black Shuck roams the Suffolk coast and the upper reaches of the Waveney. He often appears to people walking country lanes. When they try to touch him or speak to him, he either vanishes, or else the unlucky traveller finds themselves lying in a hedge or ditch. The Darkness, a rock group from Lowestoft, released a CD, *Permission to Land*, which topped the UK charts. The opening track, entitled 'Black Shuck', was an hysterical and overblown account of his activities. The story is also told by the excellent folk group The Churchfitters in the song 'Scary Dog' on their 2007 CD *Amazing*. On 27 April 1972, the *Eastern Daily Press* reported that a coastguard at Gorleston saw an unusually large black dog on the beach which suddenly vanished before his eyes. Perhaps we have not heard the last of Black Shuck.

Birds, Animals and Churches

Birds have often nested in churches: when researching this book in 2007, I found a housemartin's nest above the nave door in the porch at Rendlesham, a whitethroat's nest in the niche above the porch door at Exning and a wren's nest in the window tracery of the porch at Herringswell. In all three cases, the birds had raised young, regardless of people going to services.

Claude Ticehurst's *History of the Birds of Suffolk* (1932) mentions two wrens who took Psalm 84:3 quite literally, and nested in a floral cross in Tostock Church. In 2008 I discovered a blackbird's nest in the porch of Polstead Church. But, of all English birds, robins are best known for eccentric nesting places. In 1880 and 1931, two nested and raised young in the lectern at Blythburgh Church. To commemorate this, they are embroidered on the lectern cover and credence cloth, while a churchwarden's stave is topped with a brass shield showing a robin.

On 24 April 1949, the *Sunday Dispatch* reported that Herbert Verrells, rector of Ringsfield, had removed a robin's nest from the lectern. Three weeks later, Herbert Verrells contacted the newspaper to explain that the nest was abandoned when half completed, and he only removed it when certain the birds would not return. The following issue announced that the robins had suddenly returned to build a new nest in the lectern. *The Times* took up the story, reporting on the nestlings' progress: six babies flew on Trinity Sunday.

The *East Anglian Magazine* of July 1953 described how churchgoers at Chelsworth were bewildered by the appearance of robins. One evening a churchwarden noticed a broken window looking over the lectern. Inside he found an empty nest. The window was repaired to prevent birds re-entering, but the nest has been kept in the lectern.

Other creatures have taken advantage of church facilities. Wild bees established a colony in the tower wall of Huntingfield Church for fifty years. When they were finally removed, it

Wren's nest in the porch of Herringswell Church.

Above: *Carving of Samson, the legendary Aldeburgh Cat, on the choir stalls in the parish church.*

Right: *Father Peter McLeod Miller and his two pet donkeys, Hollie Berry and Violetta, adding life to the 2007 Palm Sunday Service in Risby Church.*

was found that they had filled a 5ft putlog (scaffolding) hole with honeycomb. On 31 March 2001, the *East Anglian Daily Times* reported that a squirrel had entered the belfry at Spexhall, knocked over the tin in which communion wafers were stored, and eaten them, leaving none for the Sunday service. Spexhall Church authorities said squirrels had stolen communion wafers before. As a stop gap measure, wafers were being hidden under the font cover.

For devotion to a church few animals can match a cat called Samson. When Anna McVittie De Bailetti moved to Aldeburgh, Samson moved into her home and adopted her as an owner. A frequent visitor to local public buildings, he regularly attended church services and functions for ten years. His exploits are described in Anna's wonderful book *Samson's Story: The Legend Of An Aldeburgh Cat* (proceeds of which go to the church and Peruvian wildlife projects). He is honoured by a wooden carving on the choir stalls of Aldeburgh Church. Standing among memorials to local poets and musicians, the Garret family and the lifeboat service, Samson has won himself a place in a pantheon of Suffolk heroes.

INDEX OF SUFFOLK
TOWNS & VILLAGES